Choosing
the Best Way
of Life

Many sincere persons would like to find a way of life that brings peace and contentment now and assures the enjoyment of a secure future. This book has been published in the hope that it will aid honest-hearted ones to identify the truly superior course of life and then to pursue it.
—The Publishers

Publishers:
WATCHTOWER BIBLE AND TRACT SOCIETY
OF NEW YORK, INC.
INTERNATIONAL BIBLE STUDENTS ASSOCIATION
Brooklyn, New York, U.S.A.

First Edition
2,000,000 Copies

Made in the United States of America

CONTENTS

NOTE: Unless otherwise indicated, Bible quotations in this book are from the modern-language *New World Translation of the Holy Scriptures,* revised edition of 1971.

Making the Right Choice

A LIFE with true meaning—how satisfying that can be! And especially if it holds promise of a secure and happy future. Can we personally choose such a way of life? There is sound reason for believing that we can.

² It is essential, however, to make that choice without delay. For one thing, our human life-span covers at most only a few decades, and it holds many uncertainties. Who can count on being able to spend many years trying out first this approach to life and then that one, hoping eventually to find the best way? Choices made may seem good—at the time. But how often do we hear it said: 'If I could only do it all over again'? Not only this, but there is reason to believe that time is limited for the human race as a whole to find the way to make the right choice.

HELP IN FINDING THE WAY

³ The question is, then, who can tell us just what will make our life really meaningful? Who can point us to a way that will result in no regrets, one that definitely assures a happy, secure future? Logically, should it not be the One who made mankind? Certainly our Creator knows the way of life that is best for us. And he reveals this to us in his inspired Word. But he does not force

1. What way of life would be truly satisfying?
2. With reference to life, why is there an urgency about making the right choice?
3. Who can tell us about what makes life really meaningful, and why?

5

us to adopt it. Rather, he warmly appeals to people of all races to make a wise choice.

⁴ Centuries ago, he began using devoted, unselfish men and women to make this appeal. His own example in generously providing all that is needed for life adds force to his entreaty. God is truly interested in us—all of us—and is ready to help us. This was made clear in these inspired words of the apostle Paul directed to people in ancient Athens:

> "The God that made the world and all the things in it, being, as this One is, Lord of heaven and earth, does not dwell in handmade temples, neither is he attended to by human hands as if he needed anything, because he himself gives to all persons life and breath and all things. And he made out of one man every nation of men . . . for them to seek God, if they might grope for him and really find him, although, in fact, he is not far off from each one of us. For by him we have life and move and exist, even as certain ones of the poets among you have said, 'For we are also his progeny.'" —Acts 17:24-28.

⁵ As the "offspring" of our Creator, what choice do we all face? The continuing words of the inspired address point to it, saying:

> "Seeing, therefore, that we are the progeny of God, we ought not to imagine that the Divine Being is like gold or silver or stone, like something sculptured by the art and contrivance of man. True, God has overlooked the times of such ignorance, yet now he is telling mankind that they should all everywhere repent. Because he has set a day in which he purposes to judge the inhabited earth in righteousness by a man whom he has appointed, and he has furnished a guarantee to all men that he has resurrected him from the dead." (Acts 17:29-31)

---

4. How has the Creator encouraged humans to make a wise choice respecting their life?

5, 6. What choices have been set before mankind?

In harmony with this, there basically are just two choices: People can choose to turn to the Most High and submit to his will; or they can choose to continue living a life that ignores him and his guidelines for happy living. What would our turning to God include?

[6] Most importantly, it includes accepting the one through whom he "purposes to judge the inhabited earth in righteousness." This is his own Son who, on earth, bore the name of Jesus. (John 5:22, 27) Why him? Because humankind is undeniably in bondage, in enslavement to imperfection, sin and death, and this one proved to be the long-awaited Messiah or Christ through whom the Most High purposes to bring freedom from that enslavement.—Isaiah 53:7-12.

[7] Here is what the Bible account shows: In the spring of 33 C.E., Jesus died on an executional stake. His death provided the needed sacrifice to atone for our sins. (1 Peter 2:24; 1 John 2:2) Forty days after being raised from the dead, he ascended to the heavens, there to present the value of his sacrifice to the Father. From then on, mankind everywhere needed to learn that freedom from sin and death could be gained *only* by accepting Jesus as God's appointed Savior. "There is no salvation in anyone else, for there is not another name under heaven that has been given among men by which we must get saved." (Acts 4:12) Hence, the desirable course of life is that which gains for us an approved standing with God as followers of his Son, yes, as *genuine* Christians.

---

7. How is Jesus Christ involved in a person's choosing the best way of life?

THE BENEFITS THAT COME FROM SUCH A LIFE

[8] Hundreds of millions today claim to be Christians. Does this mean that they have found the best way of life? No, for the mere *profession* of being Christian does not guarantee such a life. In fact, Jesus said that many would claim him as their Lord but that he would say to them: "I never knew you! Get away from me, you workers of lawlessness." (Matthew 7:23) If we profess to be Christians, we have good reason to examine whether we genuinely conform to the example and teaching of God's Son. This gives rise to the question, What should we expect to see about the way in which genuine Christians live that makes it the best course of life even now? The answer to this question is basic in determining what group among the many professed believers in Jesus Christ represents his true congregation.

[9] The Son of God said: "By this all will know that you are my disciples, if you have love among yourselves." (John 13:35) The true Christian congregation, therefore, must be an international brotherhood, free from racial, national, tribal, social and economic barriers. In that brotherhood, wherever we may go on earth, we should be able to find loyal friends, persons in whom we can confide and to whom we can entrust our belongings. Though not even being acquainted with us personally, they would show greater concern and affection for us than many of our own relatives would. (Mark 10:29, 30) To millions of professing Christians, it may sound unbelievable

---

8. Why does a person's professing to be a Christian not necessarily mean that he has found the best way of life?
9. What quality identifies the true Christian congregation, and how is this quality expressed?

that such an international brotherhood exists. But many thousands of Jehovah's Witnesses can testify to the fact that they have experienced true brotherly affection.

¹⁰ Who would not agree that enjoying good relations also with family members, neighbors and fellow workers contributes tremendously to our personal happiness? Jesus Christ lived and taught the way of love. This way builds good relations with others, for "love does not work evil to one's neighbor." (Romans 13:8-10) Then, too, when we treat others with kindness, compassion and love, we make it easier for them to display those desirable qualities toward us.

¹¹ Bible guidelines can shield us from harming ourselves. Surely we should expect this from the best way of life. Following the Bible's moral standards protects us from the emotional hurts and fears that inevitably accompany illicit relationships. (Proverbs 5:3-11, 18; Matthew 5:27, 28; Hebrews 13:4) Living as devoted disciples of Jesus Christ gives us the needed strength to stay away from heavy drinking, overeating, drug abuse, gambling and other vices. (Proverbs 23:29, 30; Isaiah 65:11; 1 Corinthians 6:9-11; 2 Corinthians 7:1) Resources formerly wasted on such habits can be used to benefit others, resulting in our experiencing the superior happiness that comes from wholehearted giving. (Acts 20:35) Following the Bible's counsel to avoid bitter resentment and envy actually promotes better health.—Psalm 37:1-5; Proverbs 14:30.

---

10. How does copying the example of Jesus Christ contribute to our enjoying good relations with others?
11. How do the Bible's guidelines protect us from harming ourselves?

[12] All of us, of course, at one time or another fall short of being the kind of person we would like to be. Either in word or in deed, we may hurt others. The fact that we are imperfect humans is painfully brought home to us. Yet, when we humbly ask God for forgiveness, he grants this to us on the basis of our heartfelt sorrow and our faith in the atoning benefits of Jesus' sacrifice. (1 John 2:1, 2) That is why we can continue to enjoy a clean conscience. We do not fear to approach God for help with any matter, confident that he will, by means of his spirit, aid us in dealing successfully with our problems and trials. —1 John 3:19-22.

[13] What of persons who choose to live a life that shows little concern for the Creator's Word? They bear their problems and afflictions alone. Aside from the possibility of enjoying a few years of life now, they have no real hope for the future. As death approaches, they often experience a fearful expectation of possible punishment from a higher power.

[14] How different it is with genuine disciples of Jesus Christ! They do not fear a future day of reckoning. Rather, with eager anticipation, they look forward to Jesus Christ's coming in glory as a victorious king who will deliver them from all injustices and oppression and then extend his rule to every part of the earth. (2 Thessalonians 1:6-10; Revelation 19:11-16; compare Psalm 72:8.) Yes, a grand future lies ahead. What will then be enjoyed?

---

12. Despite our imperfections, how can we continue to have a clean conscience?
13. What is the situation of those who have little regard for the Creator's Word?
14. To what event do genuine disciples of Jesus Christ look forward with keen anticipation?

A SUPERIOR HOPE FOR THE FUTURE

[15] The Bible answers: "There are new heavens and a new earth that we are awaiting according to his promise, and in these righteousness is to dwell." (2 Peter 3:13) "[God] will wipe out every tear from their eyes, and death will be no more, neither will mourning nor outcry nor pain be anymore. The former things have passed away." (Revelation 21:4) Not even death can prevent the realization of this future, for the Creator of life can also resurrect the dead. And he will do so by means of his Son.—John 5:28, 29.

[16] What can the fulfillment of the divine promises mean for you? Think of living under the flawless rulership of Jesus Christ among persons who genuinely care for you, who gladly put your interests ahead of their own. With all obeying the supreme law of love, there will be no crime, no injustice, no oppression. You will disappoint neither yourself nor others. Mental anguish over uncertainties or grave dangers will be unknown. The depression, emptiness and loneliness that have made life bitter for millions will be no more. The groaning due to great physical pain will never be heard. Tears of sorrow will not fill the eyes of anyone. Not even death will harm you, cutting short your activities or tearing loved ones away from you.—Isaiah 25:6-8; 65:17.

[17] Contrast this with what people have who, even though not being morally corrupt, make no room for the Creator in their lives. They may have the honor and the material possessions that they desire, perhaps find a measure of satisfaction

---

15, 16. What glorious future is in store for faithful servants of God?
17. Why is the life of those who make no room for the Creator not truly meaningful?

in helping the needy and enjoy cultural activities and wholesome pleasures. Yet, they must admit the inescapable fact that nothing in this world has any real permanence. No one is immune to accidents, disease or death. Possessions will neither protect against these things nor can they be taken along when life ends. (Psalm 49:6-20; Ecclesiastes 5:13-15; 8:8) Well-meaning efforts to help fellow humans may come to frustration because of unfavorable circumstances. So it might well be asked: How meaningful can a life be if the ultimate future it offers is just the grave? How can it be good if it actually works against a person's *eternal* future?—Compare Ecclesiastes 1:11, 15, 18; 2:10, 11; 9:11, 12.

A TIME FOR CHOOSING

[18] Especially since there is to be a day of reckoning, it is imperative for people everywhere to choose a way of life that will bring rewards, not condemnation. There is an urgency about making this choice. We do not know what tomorrow may bring. Additionally, the coming of Jesus Christ to extend his royal rule over the whole earth is drawing ever closer. The position of mankind is like that of the patriarch Noah in the days before the global deluge. He had two choices: (1) adopting the lawless ways of his contemporaries or (2) submitting to God's will. Happily, Noah made the right choice. He built an ark and, with seven members of his family, entered it at divine direction. These eight members of the human family survived the flood, and that is why we are alive today.—1 Peter 3:20.

---

18. (a) Why should we not delay in making the right choice respecting our life? (b) How is our position like that of the patriarch Noah?

[19] Similarly, for us, one of the requirements for gaining everlasting life is to make a commitment to serve Jehovah God as disciples of Jesus Christ. Just as there was no salvation outside the ark, for us there is no salvation apart from God's provision through his Son, Jesus Christ. After referring to the deliverance experienced by the eight humans in the ark, the Christian apostle Peter wrote:

"That which corresponds to this is also now saving you, namely, baptism, (not the putting away of the filth of the flesh, but the request made to God for a good conscience,) through the resurrection of Jesus Christ. He is at God's right hand, for he went his way to heaven; and angels and authorities and powers were made subject to him."—1 Peter 3:21, 22.

[20] It is not water baptism alone that results in salvation. While water can wash away filth or dirt, it is "not the putting away of the filth of the flesh" by a solemn external washing that saves. Note that Peter said that salvation is "through the resurrection of Jesus Christ." Hence, the individual who is baptized needs to acknowledge that everlasting life is only possible because the Son of God died a sacrificial death, was resurrected on the third day and finally was exalted to the right hand of God.—Romans 10:9, 10.

[21] Furthermore, the apostle Peter put the emphasis on a "request made to God for a good conscience." To come into possession of such a good conscience, all who wish to get baptized first need to repent of their past wrongdoing, exercise

---

19. What does 1 Peter 3:21, 22 reveal about salvation?
20. What shows that water baptism alone is not enough for one to gain everlasting life?
21. How does a person get a "good conscience"?

faith in God's provision for everlasting life, turn around from a bad course and dedicate or commit themselves fully to the doing of the divine will. Baptism is the public symbol of this inward resolve. After following through on what Jehovah God now requires, the baptized disciple comes into possession of a good conscience. As long as he maintains that good conscience he is in a saved condition. God's adverse judgment will not be expressed against him.—Compare Acts 2:38-40; 3:19; 10:34-48.

[22] The sooner persons choose this superior way of life, the sooner they will begin to reap its benefits. Once the choice is made to conform to God's will and submit to water baptism in symbol of our commitment or dedication, we certainly want to stick faithfully to that decision. But what will help us to continue choosing to pursue this way of life? How can we resist the influences that could result in our losing out on the present and future blessings associated with being genuine disciples of God's Son? Long ago, the inspired apostle Peter provided excellent answers to these questions. His two letters constitute the basis for what is presented in this publication. It is hoped that, by our examining these letters, we will be encouraged to embrace the best way of life as servants of God and to keep on enjoying this course of life in fuller measure.

---

22. How can we benefit from the two inspired letters of the apostle Peter?

2

Encouraging Aid to Stick to Our Decision

"NO MAN that has put his hand to a plow and looks at the things behind is well fitted for the kingdom of God." (Luke 9:62) To plow effectively, to make the furrows line up, a plowman has to keep his eyes on a fixed point at the other end of the field. How much more important it is to keep our eyes on our life's goal! Then the precious days and years of our life-span will display a pattern that is consistent with the goal for which we are aiming.

² The words of God's Son quoted above show that, once we make a commitment to serve our Creator, we should be determined to stick to that decision, come what may. The world may offer what seems to be a more alluring course—the pursuit of pleasures, popularity or material possessions. But to look back longingly to any of these things—worse, to let them become the focal point of our lives—could mean the loss of the prize we seek. It could result in a wasted life.

³ "Better is the end afterward of a matter than its beginning," says Ecclesiastes 7:8. So, while making a start in our chosen course is essential, it is the finish that really counts. That is why,

---

1, 2. (a) How did Jesus Christ illustrate the importance of sticking to our decision to serve God? (b) Why is it unwise to disregard Jesus' counsel?
3. What is a basic objective of our faith?

15

in God's Word, so much stress is placed on proving faithful to the end. (Matthew 24:13) Our faith has as a basic objective, purpose or goal, the securing of salvation or everlasting life. —1 Peter 1:9.

⁴ What can help us to persevere as loyal disciples of God's Son? For one thing, we need to see clearly, feel deeply, the precious worth of the salvation we seek. The inspired words of the apostle Peter, a close associate of Jesus Christ, can greatly aid us in this regard. His admonition can help us to see that our final salvation is something for which we should gladly endure all the pressure of opposition, no matter how severe. It is something for which we should be willing to work, to sacrifice, yes, to die if need be. (Luke 14:26-33) At 1 Peter 1:10-12, the apostle writes:

> "Concerning this very salvation a diligent inquiry and a careful search were made by the prophets who prophesied about the undeserved kindness meant for you. They kept on investigating what particular season or what sort of season the spirit in them was indicating concerning Christ when it was bearing witness beforehand about the sufferings for Christ and about the glories to follow these. It was revealed to them that, not to themselves, but to you, they were ministering the things that have now been announced to you through those who have declared the good news to you with holy spirit sent forth from heaven."

A MATTER OF INTENSE INTEREST TO PROPHETS

⁵ Centuries before Jesus' days on earth, the Hebrew prophets were inspired to foretell the suffering that would befall the promised Messiah

---

4. (a) To remain faithful, what view of salvation is important? (b) What does 1 Peter 1:10-12 tell us about the interest of the prophets in the divine arrangement for salvation?
5. What did the prophets foretell about Messiah's sufferings?

or Christ. The prophecy of Daniel specified the time for the arrival of the Christ and indicated that he would be cut off in death after a ministry of three and a half years. (Daniel 9:24-27) From Isaiah's prophecy we learn that the Messiah would be rejected and come to be a stone of stumbling. (Isaiah 8:14, 15; 28:16; 53:3) That prophecy also showed that he would carry the sicknesses of the people, be tried and condemned but remain silent before his accusers, would be spit on, numbered with sinners, pierced, die a sacrificial death and carry away sins in order to pave the way for many to gain a righteous standing with God. (Isaiah 50:6; 53:4-12) The prophecy of Zechariah pointed to Messiah's being betrayed for 30 silver pieces. (Zechariah 11:12) And the prophet Micah foretold that the Christ, the "judge of Israel," would be struck on the cheek.—Micah 5:1.

6 Among the statements in the Psalms applying to Jesus Christ are the following: He would be betrayed by an intimate associate. (Psalm 41:9) Rulers, supported by their subjects, would range themselves up against him. (Psalm 2:1, 2) The Jewish religious builders would reject him. (Psalm 118:22) False witnesses would testify against the Messiah. (Psalm 27:12) On arriving at the place of execution, he would be offered a stupefying drink. (Psalm 69:21a) Those fastening him to the stake would be 'at his hands and his feet' like wild beasts. (Psalm 22:16) Lots would be cast over his garments. (Psalm 22:18) His enemies would mock him with the words: "He committed himself to Jehovah. Let Him provide him with escape! Let him deliver him, since he has taken

---

6. What details about Messiah's sufferings are set forth in the Psalms?

delight in him!'" (Psalm 22:8) Suffering from great thirst, he would ask for a drink and be offered sour wine. (Psalms 22:15; 69:21b) Just before his death, he would cry out: "My God, my God, why have you left me?"—Psalm 22:1.

⁷ As Peter points out, the prophets were also inspired to speak of the 'glories that would follow' Messiah's suffering. By God's majestic power, this faithful Son would be raised from the dead. (Psalm 16:8-10) On his ascension to heaven, he would be seated at God's right hand, waiting until his enemies would be placed as a stool for his feet. (Psalm 110:1) He would occupy the position of an everlasting priest after the order of Melchizedek. (Psalm 110:4) His Father, "the Ancient of Days," would grant him kingly authority. (Daniel 7: 13, 14) The time would finally come for God's anointed one to dash to pieces all nations opposing his rulership. (Psalm 2:9) He would then exercise dominion over the whole earth.—Psalm 72:7, 8; Zechariah 9:9, 10.

⁸ Yes, the prophecies provided splendid fore-gleams of the Messiah's role in the divine arrangement for salvation or liberation from sin and death. His faithfulness under suffering, his death, resurrection and ascension to heaven as a glorious spirit person—all of these were needed for individuals to receive the foretold "undeserved kindness," including forgiveness of sins and total reconciliation with Jehovah God as his sons. The prophets themselves could not fully understand how salvation would come through the Messiah. Nonetheless, as the apostle Peter shows, they

---

7. What do the prophecies reveal about the "glories to follow" Christ's sufferings?
8. How did the prophets show intense interest in what they wrote, and why did they do so?

were intensely interested in the things that they had recorded. They diligently examined the prophetic words, repeatedly studying their own prophecies to discover the significance of what they had been inspired to write. Recognizing that there were marvelous truths incorporated in the revelations that they had received, the prophets used their mental faculties to the full in an effort to gain the greatest benefit from the God-given predictions. This was despite the fact that it was not until the coming of the Messiah that individuals could be recipients of the foretold unmerited kindness. Nevertheless, what the prophets understood was enough to sustain them and it also incited them to want to know still more. They were especially interested in knowing about the conditions that would exist at the time of Messiah's appearance, yes, in what "sort of season" he would undergo the foretold suffering and then experience exaltation.

⁹ As Peter made clear, the Hebrew prophets came to understand that the Messianic prophecies were not primarily recorded for their profit but for the benefit of those who would actually be living at the time of Messiah's appearance. (1 Peter 1:12) Regarding the revelations that he received, the prophet Daniel admitted: "I heard, but I could not understand." (Daniel 12:8) However, persons who accepted the "good news" that was proclaimed in the first century C.E. were the ones who profited fully from the inspired words about Messiah's first coming. It was to them that the prophets were actually ministering.—Matthew 13:16, 17.

---

9. Who especially benefited from the prophecies about the Messiah?

¹⁰ How, then, should our knowing about the intense interest of the prophets affect us? It should make us examine ourselves to see whether we have the *same concern* about salvation. Is our remaining approved servants of Jehovah God and Jesus Christ the *main object* in life? Are we truly intense about this matter? Certainly, we have good reason to be totally absorbed in proving ourselves to be loyal disciples of God's Son. The Messiah came centuries ago. His sacrificial death provided the very basis for salvation and made certain the fulfillment of every single promise of God. (2 Corinthians 1:20) The passage of time in no way weakens the certainty of the fulfillment of the divine promises. Rather, it confirms that God's desire is for as many as possible to gain salvation. (1 Timothy 2:3, 4; 2 Peter 3:9) So, with confidence, we can look forward to inheriting the blessings that the Most High has in store for faithful ones.

WHY ANGELS ARE INTERESTED

¹¹ The example of the angels should also serve to encourage us to do our utmost to remain in God's favor. Though having no personal need for the divine arrangement of salvation, faithful angels take a real interest in the outworking of God's grand purpose for humankind. The apostle Peter wrote: "Into these very things [that occupied the attention of the Hebrew prophets] angels are desiring to peer." (1 Peter 1:12) Yes, before the coming of Jesus Christ to this earth,

---

10. How should we be affected by the interest that the Hebrew prophets showed in salvation, and why?
11. According to 1 Peter 1:12, how intense is the interest of the angels in the divine arrangement for salvation?

the angels were desirous of knowing more about Christ's sufferings, the "glories to follow these" and the impact of the "good news" on mankind. The apostle Peter could speak of them as "desiring to peer" into these matters. In the original Greek, the expression "to peer" suggests a stooping down with a view to scrutinizing an object more closely. But why were the angels so keenly interested in making a careful examination of Jehovah God's revelation about salvation? As perfect spirit persons, why should the provisions for sinful, earthly humans particularly concern them?

[12] Since the angels are not all-knowing, they doubtless increase their knowledge by studiously considering God's dealings and revelations. The arrangement for the redemption of the human race truly furnished a marvelous example of Jehovah's love, justice, mercy and wisdom. Hence, by occupying themselves with gaining greater understanding of Jehovah's arrangement for saving sinful mankind, the angels would come to appreciate their heavenly Father even more. They would learn things about his personality and ways that could not be discerned from a study or an examination of any other development in the universe.—Compare Ephesians 3:8-10.

[13] Furthermore, the angels have a "fondness" for the human race. (Compare Proverbs 8:22-31.) They want to see mankind reconciled with the heavenly Father, Jehovah. That is why Jesus Christ could say: "Joy arises among the angels of God over one sinner that repents."—Luke 15:10.

12, 13. How might we explain the great interest of the angels in the salvation of mankind?

¹⁴ Yes, millions of angels rejoiced when we ourselves came to repentance. They are very much interested in seeing us maintain faithfulness to the very end. In effect, they are 'cheering us on.' May we not let our vision of the great heavenly host that have deep concern and affection for us become dim. Surely we want their joy respecting us to continue. This requires that we heed Peter's admonition: "Hence brace up your minds for activity, keep your senses completely; set your hope upon the undeserved kindness that is to be brought to you at the revelation of Jesus Christ." —1 Peter 1:13.

BRACING UP OUR MINDS FOR ACTIVITY

¹⁵ What does it mean for us to 'brace up the mind for activity'? A literal translation of the apostle Peter's words would be: "Gird up the loins of your mind." In the days of the apostle, men wore long robes. When working or engaging in vigorous activity such as running, a man would pull up the robe between his legs and fasten it securely by means of a girdle. "To gird up the loins" meant to be prepared for activity. For us to 'gird up the loins of the mind' would, therefore, signify having our mental faculties in a state of preparedness for discharging our Christian obligations and for bearing up under whatever trial may befall us.

¹⁶ With our mental powers in a state of readiness to continue in faithful service to God, we would

---

14. (a) What should the attitude of the angels toward our salvation help us to do? (b) What counsel of the apostle Peter should we keep in mind in order to remain faithful servants of God?
15. How are we to understand Peter's admonition to 'brace up our minds for activity'?
16. How can we show that we are 'keeping our senses completely'?

certainly be 'keeping our senses completely.' We would be balanced in our thinking, able to evaluate matters properly. Our life would show that we have our faculties in control and are not yielding to the allurements of a world alienated from Jehovah God. (1 John 2:16) Foremost in our lives would be the doing of what is pleasing in the eyes of our heavenly Father and his Son.

[17] To 'brace up our minds for activity and to keep our senses completely,' we must 'set our hope on the undeserved kindness that is to be brought to us at the revelation of Jesus Christ.' At the time that the Lord Jesus Christ comes in glory, all those with the heavenly hope who have remained his devoted disciples will become sharers in divine undeserved kindness. (1 Corinthians 1:4-9) Not only will these spirit-begotten disciples experience refreshing relief from the suffering that they have undergone at the hands of wicked men; but also those Christians with the hope of an earthly paradise will be preserved alive through the "great tribulation" that follows Christ's coming and have before them the prospect of unending earthly life. Indeed, we have good reason to keep ever before us the fulfillment of our Christian hopes, looking forward with eagerness to our being recipients of divine favor. Our confidence in the sure fulfillment of these hopes can spur us on in remaining loyal to our heavenly Father and his Son. May we set our sights firmly on the blessings that Christ's coming in glory will bring for his faithful followers. —Matthew 25:31-46.

17. (a) What is the "undeserved kindness" that will be brought to believers? (b) How do we 'set our hope on the undeserved kindness that is to be brought to us at the revelation of Jesus Christ'?

PROVING OURSELVES GOD'S OBEDIENT CHILDREN

¹⁸ In harmony with these hopes, our attitude should be that of "obedient children." The apostle Peter continued: "As obedient children, quit being fashioned according to the desires you formerly had in your ignorance." (1 Peter 1:14) As children who respect and love their heavenly Father, we should want to submit ourselves joyfully to his requirements, appreciating that this is the right thing to do. No longer do we want to conduct our affairs of life in the manner to which we were accustomed before becoming disciples of Jesus Christ. In our ignorance of God's commands, we may have indulged our sinful passions, selfishly put our own interests first to the hurt of others, or centered our lives around gaining material possessions, popularity or authority. To a large extent, we patterned our lives in harmony with the attitudes, words and actions of those around us. We now know that such a way of life that ignores God is empty, meaningless.

¹⁹ To enjoy a richness of life, we need to imitate Jehovah God, who is holy, clean or pure. Is our imitating our heavenly Father limited to formal worship? Note that the apostle Peter says: "In accord with the Holy One who called you, do you also become holy yourselves *in all your conduct.*" (1 Peter 1:15) Then he quoted from Leviticus 19:2, which reads: "You should prove yourselves holy, because I Jehovah your God am holy." (1 Peter 1:16) These words in Leviticus appear in a setting that outlines what Jehovah God required of the Israelites in conducting both their formal worship and their regular daily affairs.

18. How do we show ourselves to be "obedient children"?
19. As illustrated by the Mosaic law, what is included in being "holy"?

Included among these requirements for holy conduct are: Proper regard for parents, honesty, consideration for the deaf, the blind and other afflicted ones, not harboring grudges but loving one's fellowman, refraining from slander and from bearing false witness, and rendering justice. (Leviticus 19:3, 9-18) Really, then, no aspect of life is exempted from the requirement to be holy or pure from Jehovah's standpoint.

"CONDUCT YOURSELVES WITH FEAR"

[20] Another powerful reason for living up to our dedication to God is found in the apostle Peter's next words: "Furthermore, if you are calling upon the Father who judges impartially according to each one's work, conduct yourselves with fear during the time of your alien residence." (1 Peter 1:17) We should never lose sight of the fact that our heavenly Father, by means of his Son, will judge us. That judgment will not be influenced by outward appearances but will be impartial, in harmony with what we really are as persons. (Isaiah 11:2-4) So, if we acknowledge the Most High as our Father, we will want to conduct ourselves in such a way that he can look upon us with approval, rendering a favorable judgment toward us. We would rightly continue pursuing a course of life that reflects a healthy and reverential fear of Jehovah God.

[21] Then, too, we need to appreciate that the world and what it has to offer are temporary. We are to think of ourselves as being in an "alien residence." It is essential for us to guard against

---

20. What should we keep in mind about judgment, and how should this affect our conduct?
21. How do we show that we view our being in this world as a time of "alien residence"?

attaching ourselves to anything in this world as if it were going to continue forever. Even the once luxurious palaces of the kings of ancient Assyria, Babylon and Persia no longer provide a comfortable home for anyone; they lie in ruins. No architectural work, no product of modern engineering and technology, no painting, no sculpture, no single item manufactured by man can remain unchanged for all eternity. True, we must live in this world that is alienated from God, and we cannot "emigrate" from it. (1 Corinthians 5:9, 10) But we do not want to feel really 'at home' in the present arrangement of things. No, for we are looking forward to something far better, to the coming "new heavens and a new earth" of God's making. (2 Peter 3:13) Our journey through life in the world is a 'time of alien residence,' and our attitudes, words and actions should demonstrate that this is the case.—Compare Hebrews 11:13-16.

A PRECIOUS PRICE WAS PAID

[22] Further emphasizing the importance of our continuing to be holy, devoted servants of Jehovah God, the apostle Peter writes: "For you know that it was not with corruptible things, with silver or gold, that you were delivered from your fruitless form of conduct received by tradition from your forefathers. But it was with precious blood, like that of an unblemished and spotless lamb, even Christ's." (1 Peter 1:18, 19) Having been redeemed from the condemnation of sin and death, we are under obligation to Jehovah God who made the arrangement for our being ransomed. Suppose

---

22, 23. Why should we feel forever indebted to Jehovah God and Jesus Christ?

a large amount of silver or gold had been paid to ransom us from death. Would we not feel deeply indebted to the one who made such a major material sacrifice in our behalf?

[23] How much greater, then, is our indebtedness to Jehovah God and to Jesus Christ! The ransom price paid was far more valuable than any material treasure that can be lost, stolen or destroyed. Its value is greater than all the silver and gold found on earth today. The precious blood of the sinless Son of God is the valuable ransom price that was paid. It is the lifeblood of someone who had the right to live forever and, hence, of one who did much more than give up his life prematurely, as other men have done for what they thought to be a noble cause. The payment of this ransom price also provided the basis, as Peter says, for our being 'delivered from our fruitless form of conduct received by tradition from our forefathers.' How so?

[24] When we accepted the fact of our having been ransomed or bought with the precious blood of Jesus Christ, we abandoned our former course of life. Without knowledge of Jehovah God or his purposes, our life had been "fruitless," vain, empty, in that it revolved exclusively around the attainment of things that had no permanence. The way we conducted ourselves may even have harmed us mentally, physically and emotionally. Moreover, our parents and grandparents may have been unacquainted with the Holy Scriptures. Therefore, the standards and principles by which they conducted their affairs of life may not have been in harmony with the divine will. They may

24. Before we became disciples of Jesus Christ, how may our conduct have been "fruitless"?

even have engaged in God-dishonoring religious practices. Thus, even the "tradition" we may have received from our ancestors respecting conduct did not lead to our enjoying a purposeful life. —Compare Matthew 15:3-9.

²⁵ Surely, the words of the apostle Peter are a real encouragement for us to stick to our commitment to serve Jehovah God as devoted disciples of Jesus Christ. Never should we allow ourselves to forget about the keen interest that the Hebrew prophets and the angels showed in the divine revelations concerning salvation. May we keep ever before us the certainty of God's judgment, the fulfillment of our hope at the revelation of Jesus Christ, the importance of being clean in all our conduct because Jehovah's holiness requires it, and the fact that the period of our life in this world is but a time of alien residence. Above all, may we never, no, never, lose sight of the fact that we have been ransomed with the precious blood of Jesus Christ!

²⁶ When compared with the blessings that come from serving the Most High, the showy things of this world are really refuse. (1 Corinthians 7:29-31; Philippians 3:7, 8) No amount of money can buy a clean conscience, a meaningful life now and an abiding future of happy living. But faithful service to God does bring such blessings. What powerful reasons we have for making this our chief concern in life!

---

25. How can the words of 1 Peter 1:10-19 provide strong encouragement for us to remain faithful to Jehovah God and our Lord Jesus Christ?
26. How do the things this world can offer compare with what we gain from serving Jehovah?

3

A Hope with a Sure Guarantee

MANY people claim to believe that God exists. But to live in a way that meets divine approval requires far more than this. We need to be firmly convinced that what may come to us in the way of suffering is as nothing when compared with the grand blessings the Almighty God will bestow on his servants.

² For this reason, just to serve our Creator out of a sense of duty because of his being our Life-Giver is not sufficient either. A mere sense of duty is not strong enough to keep us faithful in view of all the trials we might face—physical and verbal abuse, sickness, disappointments, economic hardships. Only an intense, unbreakable love for our heavenly Father could do that.

³ To have that kind of love for God, we must believe that he himself is loving, good, generous. The Bible shows that such faith is absolutely essential for Christians. It says: "He that approaches God must believe that he is and that he becomes the rewarder of those earnestly seeking him." (Hebrews 11:6) Any minimizing of God's promise to bless his servants actually distorts our knowledge of him. It may hinder us from recognizing Jehovah as a God who deeply appreciates the fine works of his people. (Hebrews 6:10) On the

1-3. (a) Why is mere belief in the existence of God not enough for us to have divine approval? (b) According to Hebrews 11:6, what must we believe, and why is this important?

other hand, our firm conviction that the Most High is a rewarder creates within us an appreciative response, stirring us to want to please him.

'SAFEGUARDED FOR SALVATION'

⁴ Of course, we do not *earn* salvation by our service to God, such as by maintaining fine conduct and aiding others spiritually and materially. Our heavenly Father himself has made all the provisions for our gaining everlasting life, and he helps us to do his will and to receive that blessing. Our God-given hope, therefore, encourages us to submit ourselves fully to divine direction. Total confidence in Jehovah as a rewarder enables us to continue cooperating with him in making us genuine, fully developed Christians. (Ephesians 4:13-15) True, such active cooperation with our Maker demands that we exert ourselves to control our sinful tendencies. But he is the One who, by means of his spirit, really makes our spiritual growth possible. The following words of the apostle Peter beautifully emphasize God's part in securing the fulfillment of our Christian hope:

"Blessed be the God and Father of our Lord Jesus Christ, for according to his great mercy he gave us a new birth to a living hope through the resurrection of Jesus Christ from the dead, to an incorruptible and undefiled and unfading inheritance. It is reserved in the heavens for you, who are being safeguarded by God's power through faith for a salvation ready to be revealed in the last period of time."—1 Peter 1:3-5.

⁵ The Christians to whom these words were directed had good reason to bless Jehovah God,

---

4. How does Jehovah God help us to secure salvation, and so what should we be doing?
5. Why did first-century Christians have good reason to bless Jehovah?

and also to speak well of him or to praise him. They had been brought forth as children of the Most High by a second birth, as it were. (John 1:12, 13; 3:5-8) This "new birth" came about through the operation of the holy spirit toward them. It was not as a result of any special merit on their part that they were constituted sons of God. But it was because of the divine mercy or compassion expressed in their being forgiven of their sins. On becoming children of the Almighty, these disciples of Jesus Christ were also made heirs.

⁶ As heirs, they had the hope of receiving an inheritance. That hope, as Peter shows, is a "living hope." It is "living" in more than one way. Like God's message or word, which is "alive and exerts power," the hope is living and powerful. (Hebrews 4:12) Primarily, this is because it is a hope divinely given by the living and eternal God, and it is centered in his Son who 'dies no more.' The Son has the power of an indestructible life and is able to save completely those putting their trust in him. (Jeremiah 10:10; Habakkuk 1:12; Hebrews 7:16, 25; 1 Peter 1:23) Jesus Christ is himself the "living bread" sent by God and "if anyone eats of this bread he will live forever." (John 6:50, 51, 57) The Son gives "living water" that becomes in those receiving it a "fountain of water bubbling up to impart everlasting life." (John 4:10, 14) So, too, the "living hope" given as a result of the "new birth" is capable of carrying its possessors onward to the realization of their reward and life eternal.

---

6. What are some aspects that make the Christian hope a "living" one?

⁷ There is vitality in that hope. It is an invigorating, energizing force in the life of those cherishing it. This hope affects their whole life, makes itself evident in the way they use their life. Like true faith, such a hope cannot be dead, with no fruitage, no activity to demonstrate its existence. (James 2:14-26) It is a spirited hope that enlivens us, and we are encouraged, supported and strengthened by its comfort and by its unshakable certainty of fulfillment.

⁸ Far different, then, from the hopes of those putting their trust in imperfect, dying men, this hope is not a dead hope that will come to disappointment because of lacking any solid basis. It cannot fail to be realized. Jehovah's unchangeable promise, coupled with his matchless power to fulfill it, serves as a sure foundation for the Christian hope.—Compare Isaiah 55:10, 11; Hebrews 6:13-20.

⁹ The apostle Peter links this "living hope" with "the resurrection of Jesus Christ from the dead." When God's Son was impaled on the stake and his disciples saw him die, their hope virtually died with him. But when the evidence of his resurrection reached them, their hope was revived, took on new life, 'caught fire' and impelled them to bear witness. (Luke 24:13-34; Acts 4: 20) Because he was raised to spirit life, the Son of God could present the value of his sacrifice, the redemption price, to the Father. Had Jesus Christ not been resurrected, no one could have been

---

7. How does the "living hope" affect its possessors?
8. Because it is a "living hope," what can be said about its being fulfilled?
9. What has made this "living hope" possible?

redeemed from sin and death. (1 Corinthians 15:14-19) Apart from his resurrection, there could have been no "living hope."

¹⁰ The grand inheritance to which the apostle Peter and his fellow believers looked forward is 'incorruptible, undefiled and unfading.' Being incorruptible, it cannot be destroyed or damaged in any way. No defilement or pollution could become attached to it, for it cannot be obtained through any scheming, deceit or other lawless means. That wonderful inheritance will never fall into the hands of unprincipled men. Furthermore, unlike lovely flowers that soon lose their beauty and brilliance, throughout all eternity the inheritance will never fade in its grandeur and attractiveness.

¹¹ According to Peter's words, the promised inheritance is "reserved in the heavens." It is sure for Christ's joint heirs. There in the heavens, it is more thoroughly protected and preserved than in any bank vault, because the invisible heavens are the permanent abiding place of the eternal God, Jehovah. (Psalms 103:19; 115:3, 16; Matthew 5:11, 12) Furthermore, the apostle Peter pointed out that the Almighty would help them to receive their inheritance. The Most High, by means of his spirit, would exercise his "power" toward them, aiding them to remain acceptable before him, protecting their life interests. As a result, "in the last period of time," they would not share in the condemnatory judgment passed on faithless ones but would be saved for everlasting life.

---

10. Why could Peter refer to the inheritance as being 'incorruptible, undefiled and unfading'?
11. Why is the "inheritance" secure?

¹² Like first-century Christians, all believers today can be confident that Jehovah God will safeguard them for salvation. By means of his holy
spirit, he initially made it possible for us to have
faith and, by the same spirit, he will continue to
strengthen our faith. This faith can carry us
through all manner of trials successfully. (1 John
5:4) Do we not have sound reasons, then, to be
thankful for what Jehovah God continues to do
in aiding us to secure everlasting life? Indeed, and
especially when we consider that this is not due
to any merit on our part but because of Jehovah's
great mercy.

DEATH CANNOT PREVENT
THE REALIZATION OF OUR HOPE

¹³ Not even death can prevent our seeing the
fulfillment of our Christian hope. What our heavenly Father did in connection with his Son provides a sure, unfailing guarantee that our hope
rests on a firm basis. The apostle Peter wrote:

"True, he [God's Son] was foreknown before the
founding of the world, but he was made manifest
at the end of the times for the sake of you who
through him are believers in God, the one who
raised him up from the dead and gave him glory;
so that your faith and hope might be in God."
—1 Peter 1:20, 21.

¹⁴ Before Adam and Eve founded a world of
mankind by having children, Jehovah God determined that his only-begotten Son would be
the one to redeem the human race from enslavement to sin and death. (Compare Genesis 3:15;

---

12. How will Jehovah God "safeguard" us for salvation?
13. What guarantees that our Christian hope rests on a solid
foundation?
14. How was Jesus Christ "foreknown before the founding of
the world" and "made manifest at the end of the times"?

4:1, 2; Luke 11:49-51.) With the coming of the Messiah, the Jewish system of things, including its priesthood, sacrifices and temple services, entered its last days. Messiah's arrival did mark the start of a new epoch in human history. Therefore, the apostle Peter spoke of Christ's being "made manifest *at the end of the times.*"

¹⁵ But why did the apostle say that God's Son was made manifest "for the sake of you who through him are believers in God"? Before Jesus came to the earth, no one could take advantage of the redemptive work that he would accomplish. Only in the first century could believers start doing so. By exercising faith in the Christ, these believers were also putting faith in the Father, the One who had sent the Son to this earth. (John 17:21) Furthermore, as Peter stated, what Jehovah God did for his Son—resurrecting him and giving him "glory" by exalting him to his own right hand—provides sound reason for putting our faith and hope in the Almighty. How so?

¹⁶ Just as the Most High raised his Son, he can also resurrect others of his servants. Since Jesus Christ was raised to immortal heavenly life, his first-century disciples could be sure that they, too, would share with him in celestial glory. The resurrection of God's Son stands as an unchangeable guarantee that humans who are sleeping in death will be raised to life.—1 Corinthians 15: 12-22.

¹⁷ That is why the fact of Jesus' resurrection needed to be well established, and it was. There were upward of 500 disciples who saw the resur-

15. Why could Peter say that Jesus Christ was made manifest "for the sake of you who through him are believers in God"?
16. Of what is the resurrection of Jesus Christ a guarantee?
17. How well established is the resurrection of Jesus Christ?

rected Son of God. (1 Corinthians 15:6) These eyewitnesses knew that God's enemies might take away their freedom and even kill them if they presented testimony regarding this grand miracle. Yet, faithful disciples of Jesus Christ witnessed to this fact with all boldness. (Compare Acts 4:1-3; 7:52-60.) Such courageous faith was only possible because they had solid evidence of his resurrection.

CHRIST'S COMING IN GLORY IS SURE

¹⁸ As in the case of the resurrection of his Son, Jehovah God also saw to it that clear testimony was provided respecting the certainty of Christ's coming "with power and great glory." (Matthew 24:30; Revelation 1:7) The apostle Peter said:

"No, it was not by following artfully contrived false stories that we acquainted you with the power and presence of our Lord Jesus Christ, but it was by having become eyewitnesses of his magnificence. For he received from God the Father honor and glory, when words such as these were borne to him by the magnificent glory: 'This is my son, my beloved, whom I myself have approved.' Yes, these words we heard borne from heaven while we were with him in the holy mountain." (2 Peter 1:16-18)

To what event was Peter here referring?

¹⁹ It was to the transfiguration of the Lord Jesus Christ. Sometime after Passover of 32 C.E., the Son of God told his disciples: "Truly I say to you that there are some of those standing here that will not taste death at all until first they see the Son of man coming in his kingdom."

---

18. What does the apostle Peter indicate about "the power and presence of our Lord Jesus Christ"?
19. When and how did Peter, James and John become eye-witnesses of Christ's magnificence?

(Matthew 16:28) In a matter of days, those words of Jesus were fulfilled. Taking with him the apostles Peter, James and John, God's Son climbed a high mountain, presumably Hermon. On a spur of this mountain, the following took place: "[Jesus] was transfigured before them, and his face shone as the sun, and his outer garments became brilliant as the light." Thus the three apostles had confirmed to them that Jesus' coming in Kingdom power would indeed be glorious. Then a "bright cloud" formed and a voice came out of it, saying: "This is my Son, the beloved, whom I have approved; listen to him."—Matthew 17:1-5.

20 Faith in Jesus' arrival in Kingdom power, therefore, was not based on false stories originating with men. No trickery or deceit was involved in trying to persuade others to accept the belief that the Son of God would return "with power and great glory." Peter, James and John saw Jesus Christ glorified before their very eyes, and they heard God's own voice sounding forth from the bright cloud or the "magnificent glory." This voice acknowledged Jesus as being the beloved Son. The acknowledgment and the brilliant appearance that was then granted him were truly a bestowal of honor and glory on Jesus. Because of this grand divine revelation from Jehovah, Peter rightly referred to the mountain where the transfiguration took place as "the holy mountain."

21 Of what import should this transfiguration be to believers? Peter answers: "Consequently we have the prophetic word made more sure; and you are doing well in paying attention to it as

to a lamp shining in a dark place, until day dawns and a daystar rises, in your hearts." (2 Peter 1:19) Yes, the transfiguration vision verifies the prophetic word about the coming of the Lord Jesus Christ in Kingdom power. This vision provided a foregleam of his kingly glory. Of course, apart from power or authority, there can be no royal glory, magnificence or dignity. Hence, the transfiguration also served to establish the certainty of Jesus' coming in power.

²² We today 'do well' in giving heed to the prophetic word, for nothing could be more vital to our life interests, could result in greater or more lasting benefits. People may avidly read world news, examine predictions by political, economic and scientific experts and, in the end, find that they have gotten nowhere. But the light shining from the prophetic word will never lead us down a dead-end road or leave us in a confusing maze of conflicting signposts and directions. So this prophetic word merits an important place in our study and meditation. We are wise to avail ourselves of all opportunities to assemble with fellow believers when the "word" is discussed. But our "paying attention" involves more than careful reading or respectful listening. It means *acting* on the prophetic word, letting it influence our conduct, the way in which we use our time, energy and assets. (Compare James 1:22-27.) Yes, we rightly acknowledge the genuine practicality of that prophetic word in our daily life and do not view it as merely something to which we give consideration during periods of formal worship.

22, 23. (a) How do we show that we are "doing well" in paying attention to the prophetic word? (b) How is that word like a lamp?

²³ In harmony with Peter's urging, we should let the prophetic word serve us as a lamp shining in a dark place, illuminating our hearts. If we 'pay attention' to it by allowing it to guide us in all affairs of life, it will conduct us safely until that grand day when the "daystar," the Lord Jesus Christ, reveals himself in all his magnificent glory. (Compare Revelation 22:16.) The revelation of the Son of God will spell destruction for the faithless ones and the bestowal of grand blessings on his devoted disciples. (2 Thessalonians 1:6-10) Surely the hope that is bound up with the fulfillment of the prophetic word should encourage us to do our utmost to be found standing as approved before our Lord at his revelation. —Luke 21:34-36.

²⁴ In fact, the entire prophetic word contained in the Holy Scriptures needs to be given sober consideration and allowed to guide our life. The very nature of the prophetic word, the way it came to be written, should fill us with confidence respecting the future. Jehovah's prophets did not evaluate certain trends in human affairs and then make predictions based on their personal interpretation of these developments. The prophecies were not the conclusions that the prophets themselves reached after making a careful analysis of the then-existing conditions. No, the prophets had their minds stimulated by the holy spirit and were moved to express God's message. The apostle Peter continued: "You know this first, that no prophecy of Scripture springs from any private interpretation. For prophecy was at no time brought by man's will, but men spoke from God

24. Why can we have confidence in the entire prophetic word contained in the Bible?

as they were borne along by holy spirit." (2 Peter 1:20, 21) Because true prophecy does not originate with error-prone humans but with our all-wise Creator, we know that all prophecies set forth in God's Word will be fulfilled.

²⁵ The Christian hope does rest on solid evidence. Reliable eyewitness testimony confirms that humans sleeping in death will be raised to life and that Jesus Christ will manifest his glory and power. Grand will be that day when our Lord takes action against all who refuse to serve the Creator and delivers his faithful followers from all suffering, bringing in a righteous new order free from sickness, pain and death.—Revelation 21:4, 5.

25. What can we say about the surety of our Christian hope?

4

Food That Is Essential for Everlasting Life

TO A hungry, famished person, even a taste of honey can bring renewed strength, can make his eyes shine. Of the things set forth in God's Word, it is rightly said that they are "sweeter than honey and the flowing honey of the combs." This is because of the tremendous benefits that divine guidelines bring to the lives of those receiving them with appreciation. (1 Samuel 14:27; Psalms 19:9-11; 119:103) For those gaining the wisdom set forth in the inspired Word, "there exists a future, and [their] own hope will not be cut off."—Proverbs 24:13, 14.

² We have God's promise that he will 'safeguard his servants for life everlasting,' doing this by means of his spirit. (1 Peter 1:5) This is certainly encouraging. But we are mistaken if we think this comes with no effort required on the part of those so helped. God's spirit can work to the good of any of us only to the extent that we cooperate with it, and such cooperation includes feeding on the inspired Scriptures. The Son of God showed why this is so.

³ Explaining to his disciples how God's spirit would aid them, Jesus said: "The helper, the holy

1. Why are the things set forth in God's Word like honey?
2. If God's spirit is going to accomplish good within us, what must we do?
3. What did Jesus Christ say that the spirit would do for his disciples?

41

spirit, which the Father will send in my name, that one will teach you all things and bring back to your minds all the things I told you." (John 14:26) After Jesus' returning to the heavens, the spirit, in the capacity of a remembrancer, would recall to the minds of the disciples his sayings and, as a teacher, it would enable them to *understand* the application of the things brought to mind.

⁴ Since we have never been taught personally by Jesus Christ, our situation differs from that of the apostles. However, all the vital teachings of the Son of God are preserved for us in the Bible. So, whenever necessary, the holy spirit can recall to our minds points from the inspired Scriptures and help us in discerning their correct application. Since God's spirit functions as a remembrancer and a teacher, we must cooperate with it by a careful consideration of the Bible. If our deposit of Scriptural knowledge is very limited, we cannot possibly get the full benefit from the spirit's operating in our behalf as a remembrancer and a teacher.

⁵ Then, too, the spirit is holy and, therefore, aids only those who are holy or clean from Jehovah's standpoint. That is why it is not enough merely to read the Bible or to have it read to us. There also needs to be a heartfelt desire to put away all traits that conflict with God's standard of cleanness or purity. Note how this is stressed in the following words of the apostle Peter:

---

4. How can God's spirit help us, and how does this emphasize the importance of increasing in Bible knowledge?
5. (a) To benefit fully from the operation of God's spirit, why is it important to put away bad traits? (b) What counsel did the apostle Peter give about spiritual feeding?

"Put away all badness and all deceitfulness and hypocrisy and envies and all sorts of backbiting, and, as newborn infants, form a longing for the unadulterated milk belonging to the word, that through it you may grow to salvation, provided you have tasted that the Lord is kind."—1 Peter 2:1-3.

⁶ When we diligently strive to do God's will, our minds and hearts are prepared to feed on the Scriptures. But still more is involved in developing a fine spiritual appetite. The apostle urged: "As newborn infants, *form a longing* for the unadulterated milk belonging to the word." (1 Peter 2:2) Milk totally satisfies newborn babies. They want no other food. Like such infants, new believers need the 'milk of the word' and should cultivate a real desire for it. Then, on attaining Christian maturity, they would certainly want to have a like craving for the solid spiritual food.—Hebrews 5:12-14.

⁷ Yes, regardless of the length of time that we have been walking in the way of the truth, there still is much more to be learned about our Maker and his will for us. (Compare 1 Corinthians 13: 12.) Because the Scriptures contain the thoughts of the all-wise God, Jehovah, even angels benefit from the revelations set forth therein. (1 Peter 1:12) How, then, could any human think that he can gain a complete understanding of God's holy Word within a matter of a few years? So it would be most inappropriate to content ourselves with knowing a small portion of his Word and, in effect, be telling our heavenly Father that we wish that he had been less generous with his spiritual provisions contained in the Holy Scriptures.

---

6. Who are being urged to form a longing for the "milk"?
7. Why can we not expect to have a full understanding of God's Word in a few years?

CULTIVATING A TASTE FOR SPIRITUAL FOOD

[8] Our love for Jehovah God and Jesus Christ should move us to want to understand as much of the Bible as possible. It is through the pages of the Scriptures that we are aided to come to know our heavenly Father and his Son better, drawing us closer to them. As the apostle Peter observed, we have already "tasted that the Lord is kind." (1 Peter 2:3) In expression of his love, Jesus Christ died for us and made it possible for us to have a clean standing before our heavenly Father. (John 15:13; 1 John 2:2) As a result, we can approach Jehovah God freely, committing all our cares and anxieties to him. (Hebrews 10:19-22; 1 John 3:19-22) The blessings, guidance and help that we have received as disciples of Jesus Christ amply demonstrate that our Master is kind and has great affection for us. (Matthew 11:28-30) If what we have already tasted or experienced is so good, should we not want to conform ourselves even closer to the example of Jehovah God and that of his Son? (Psalm 34:8) Careful, prayerful consideration of the Bible will help us to do just that.

[9] What if you find that your longing for the "word" is not very great? Take time, then, to think appreciatively about what Jehovah God and Jesus Christ have done in your behalf. Also, examine whether you have spoiled your spiritual appetite by giving undue attention to the philosophies, speculations and propaganda of a world alienated from God. Another enemy of a spiritual appetite is a person's largely restricting his read-

8. What should incite us to want to gain a better understanding of the Scriptures?
9. (a) What may work against a good spiritual appetite, and why so? (b) What can be done to improve our spiritual appetite?

ing to picture magazines or to material that does not require careful thought and meditation. It simply must be recognized that the Bible was written to instruct, not to entertain. While the words themselves may not be difficult, often the thoughts expressed convey a depth of meaning that can only be fathomed by taking time to reflect prayerfully on what is said.

10 The illustrations used by Jesus Christ, for example, are simple. But the vital truths that they reveal cannot be discovered merely by a casual reading of any translation of the Bible. Remember, Jews who heard the Son of God speaking in their own language did not get the full impact of what he taught. Though ordinary persons understood the words that he used, the significance of what Jesus said remained hidden even from the educated. Why? The majority of Jesus' listeners lacked humility and a longing for spiritual food. Hence, they made no further inquiry to gain real insight.—Matthew 13:13-15.

11 Certainly, we do not want to be satisfied with a superficial knowledge of the Bible, perhaps being familiar with the Bible narratives or "stories," as well as elementary doctrines. If we claim to love God and Christ, we need to be willing to spend time with the Bible, exerting ourselves to get the import, the sense and spirit of what it says and then to apply these. No worthwhile skill is gained without effort. Therefore, should we not expect to put forth great effort in order to increase our knowledge of Jehovah, the source

10. What facts about the illustrations of Jesus Christ prove that casual reading of the Scriptures is not enough for one to gain accurate knowledge?
11. Why should we not be satisfied with superficial Scriptural knowledge?

of all wisdom?—Compare Proverbs 2:1-6; 1 Timothy 4:13-16.

[12] Our attitude toward gaining a better understanding of God's Word will have a direct bearing on the blessings that will be bestowed on us. A failure to use our opportunities to the full in coming to know Jehovah God better may not necessarily result in losing our lives. But it could lead to our being guilty of not carrying out the divine will in certain respects and then losing out on blessings. In one of his illustrations, Jesus showed that ignorance will not shield a person from a measure of loss. The servant who does things deserving of strokes because of not understanding his master's will is still punished, though not as severely as the slave who, with full knowledge, deliberately disobeys. (Luke 12:47, 48) It is, therefore, a serious matter when a person fails to make room in his life for regular study of God's Word and, as a result, is not making the needed advancement in Christian conduct and activity.

[13] The entire Word of God is designed to help us to "grow to salvation," that is, to secure our final salvation as approved disciples of the Lord Jesus Christ. Hence, if we are truly interested in our eternal welfare, this should be manifest from our earnest desire to come to a better knowledge of Jehovah God and of his Son by means of the inspired Scriptures.

[14] Of course, more than our own life is involved. (Compare 1 Timothy 4:16.) As followers of Jesus

12. What bearing does our attitude toward gaining accurate knowledge have on the blessings that we may receive?
13. What can God's Word help us to secure, and how should this affect our spiritual feeding?
14. What effect can genuine interest in the spiritual welfare of others have on our spiritual appetite?

Christ, we have a commission to help others to become his disciples. (Matthew 28:19, 20) How can we do this when we are seriously lacking in Biblical understanding? Can we really say that we are genuinely interested in the spiritual welfare of others when we put forth only limited effort to increase in the very knowledge that could help them? At times the needed stimulation for improving a spiritual appetite comes when a person starts to teach someone else. Not infrequently those who increase the amount of time spent in sharing Bible truth with others find that their own desire for spiritual food is intensified. For example, questions raised by interested ones may provide the needed incentive for a person to dig deeper into the Word of God, with a view to providing satisfying answers.

[15] But what about persons who have serious difficulty in reading or who are unable to read the Scriptures for themselves? They can get the benefit of what the Bible contains by having it read and explained to them. Then they can meditate on the information they hear and can apply it in their lives. (Revelation 1:3; Nehemiah 8:8) Of course, if the problem involves limited education, it would be good for such persons to take advantage of available arrangements for learning to read or to improve their reading ability. When only some portions of the Scriptures are available in a particular language, great responsibility falls on those who are teaching others and who know languages in which the complete Bible is available. Like the apostle Paul, they should strive to make known "all the counsel of God."—Acts 20:27.

---

15. How can persons who cannot read or who have difficulty in reading benefit from what is contained in the Scriptures?

THE WORD'S EFFECT ON OUR LIVES

[16] Our prayerful consideration of God's Word, in all humility, can have a wholesome effect on our lives now. This is evident from what the apostle Peter wrote to his fellow believers:

"Now that you have purified your souls by your obedience to the truth with unhypocritical brotherly love as the result, love one another intensely from the heart. For you have been given a new birth, not by corruptible [seed that is responsible for human, fleshly existence, which is subject to death], but by incorruptible reproductive seed, through the word of the living and enduring God. For 'all flesh is like grass, and all its glory is like a blossom of grass; the grass becomes withered, and the flower falls off, but the saying of Jehovah endures forever.' Well, this is the 'saying,' this which has been declared to you as good news."—1 Peter 1:22-25.

[17] Consider how Peter's words applied to Christians in the first century C.E. When those disciples of Jesus Christ absorbed the truth of the "good news," they were moved to put forth effort to purify themselves, to cast away wrong practices. With the aid of God's spirit, they obediently conformed to what the truth required of them. As a result, they began displaying real love toward those related to them in the faith. (John 13:34, 35) However, this marvelous transformation in their lives did not come about without personal effort. Only by obediently yielding to the influence of the truth and of God's spirit could they display unhypocritical brotherly love. For this reason, Peter could urge them: "Love one another intensely from the heart." (1 Peter 1:22) The Greek word for "intensely" literally means

---

16, 17. (a) According to the apostle Peter, what impact did God's Word have on first-century Christians? (b) What shows that personal effort was required for the "word" to be truly at work in believers?

"outstretchedly." So, this display of love is not to be narrow or confined because of suspicion, envy or jealousy but is to be expressed from a pure heart. It is not a formalistic love lacking in genuine warmth but a love distinguished by intense feeling and affection. Because the God of love, Jehovah, had made such Christian disciples his sons, giving them a new birth, it was only right that they apply themselves diligently in giving proof of their sonship by manifesting intense love for their fellow believers.—1 John 3:10, 11.

[18] In the case of all disciples of Jesus Christ today, the changes that can result from feeding on and conforming to "the word of the living and enduring God" are not superficial or short-lived. That "word" is incorruptible. Hence, all who continue under the influence of the truth of the "good news" are continuously affected for good. While sinful humans, like the grass, lose their fine appearance and die, the changes effected by the enduring "word" and spirit of God remain.

[19] May we, therefore, never neglect our spiritual needs but be diligent in filling our minds and hearts with the truth. By our fine spiritual appetite we can gain spiritual health and strength. Then, as we humbly submit to the influence of the "good news" and God's holy spirit, may we prove ourselves to be faithful disciples of Jesus Christ, aiding others to come to an accurate knowledge of the Scriptures. Thus our feeding on the enduring "word" will help us to grow to salvation, securing for us an eternal future.

---

18. (a) Why are the changes that can result from conforming to God's Word not superficial or short-lived? (b) How does what is accomplished through the "word" and God's spirit differ from the experience of sinful humans?
19. How should we feel about our spiritual needs?

5

The Perfect Example—Christ

FOR us to be moved to follow someone whole-heartedly, we must believe that his example deserves to be imitated. The higher our esteem and the greater our affection for that person, the more intense will be our desire to be like him. So the extent to which we copy Jesus Christ as our model largely depends on our having deep love and appreciation for him. What will help us to grow in our affection for the Son of God?

[2] Like many who became Christians after Jesus' death in the first century, we have not personally seen the Son of God. (1 Peter 1:8) But our not beholding him with our literal eyes is no barrier to our coming to love him to an ever greater degree. Many who actually saw Jesus Christ in the flesh did not come to know him. They judged him by what they thought the Messiah should be like, and were stumbled. For example, people from his home territory said: "Where did this man get this wisdom and these powerful works? Is this not the carpenter's son? Is not his mother called Mary, and his brothers James and Joseph and Simon and Judas? And his sisters, are they not all with us? Where, then, did this man get all these things?"—Matthew 13:54-57.

---

1. What is needed for us to want to imitate Jesus Christ?
2, 3. (a) What shows that our coming to know Jesus Christ is not dependent on our literally seeing him? (b) Why did many Jews who actually saw the Son of God not come to appreciate him?

³ Truly, the eyes and ears of those who expressed themselves in this faithless way did not convey accurate information to their minds and hearts. Because they judged him by outward appearances, as being from the family of a lowly carpenter, they failed to recognize Jesus as the promised Messiah, the Son of God. The significance of Jesus' miracles was obscured in their minds. They saw his fine qualities but misjudged them.

⁴ We, on the other hand, can come to know and love Jesus Christ to a greater extent by carefully and prayerfully considering what the Scriptures tell us about him. (Compare 1 John 1:1-4.) The Bible presents a most heartwarming picture of the Son of God. Though perfect, Jesus Christ was never hypercritical or overbearing in his dealings with suffering humans. (Matthew 9:10-13) His superior wisdom did not make others feel ignorant or uncomfortable in his presence, for he was "mild-tempered and lowly in heart." (Matthew 11:29) Even children were at ease with him. (Matthew 19:13-15) Jesus Christ took into consideration the limitations of his disciples and patiently repeated vital lessons. (John 16:12) When seeing the sick and the spiritually needy, he was moved with pity and gladly came to their aid. (Matthew 9:36; Mark 6:34) His interest in the poor is shown by the fact that he and the apostles had a common fund from which they could draw to assist the needy. (John 12:4-6; 13:29) Eagerly God's Son expended himself fully in behalf of others, and courageously exposed hypocrisy and error. (Matthew 23:2-35) Finally, in proof of his great love for humankind, he gave

---

4. How can we come to know the Son of God better, and what are some things that we can learn from this source?

up his life. (John 15:13) What a superb example of courage, humility and love the Son of God set for us!

JEHOVAH'S ESTIMATION OF HIS SON

⁵ Furthermore, only the Scriptures teach us how Jehovah God regards his Son. Such knowledge about Jesus Christ could not be obtained merely by the physical senses of sight, hearing and touch. Take, for instance, the apostle Peter's words to his fellow believers about the honorable position of God's Son and the benefits that result from coming to him. The apostle wrote:

"Coming to him as to a living stone, rejected, it is true, by men, but chosen, precious, with God, you yourselves also as living stones are being built up a spiritual house for the purpose of a holy priesthood, to offer up spiritual sacrifices acceptable to God through Jesus Christ. For it is contained in Scripture: 'Look! I am laying in Zion a stone, chosen, a foundation cornerstone, precious; and no one exercising faith in it will by any means come to disappointment.'" (1 Peter 2:4-6)

What did this mean to first-century Christians?

⁶ By acknowledging Jesus Christ as their Lord and the one through whom they could gain salvation, they came to him "as to a living stone." The expression "living stone" is very fitting. Jesus Christ is not like an ordinary, cold, inanimate stone from which no life-sustaining substance can be drawn. The Son of God is like the rock-mass from which the Israelites received a miraculous supply of water in the wilderness. According to

---

5. What important knowledge about Jesus Christ cannot be obtained by the physical senses of sight, hearing and touch?
6. (a) In the first century, how did believers come to the Son of God "as to a living stone"? (b) Why is Jesus rightly called a "living stone"?

the inspired apostle Paul, "that rock-mass meant the Christ." It was a symbol or a pictorial type of the Son of God. (1 Corinthians 10:4) Jesus himself said:

> "If anyone is thirsty, let him come to me and drink." (John 7:37) "Whoever drinks from the water that I will give him will never get thirsty at all, but the water that I will give him will become in him a fountain of water bubbling up to impart everlasting life." (John 4:14)

Thus the Son of God indicated that his teaching, if taken in like refreshing water, would lead to salvation—to life without end. Moreover, Jesus Christ has also been granted life-giving power. Therefore, like his Father, he can impart life to others on the basis of his propitiatory sacrifice, raising them from the dead.—John 5:28, 29.

[7] As Peter pointed out, Jesus was "rejected, it is true, by men." Especially the proud religious leaders saw nothing in the Son of God that they regarded as worthy of imitation. They did not appreciate his exemplary compassion and love for humankind. When Jesus gave spiritual help to persons known to be sinners, the religious leaders objected: "This man welcomes sinners and eats with them." (Luke 15:2) They witnessed how the Son compassionately made use of the sabbath to open the eyes of the blind, to heal the sick and to free the crippled from their affliction. But instead of rejoicing and praising God, the religious leaders were filled with rage and plotted to kill him. (Matthew 12:9-14; Mark 3:1-6; Luke 6:7-11; 14:1-6) They told a blind man whose sight had been restored: "This is not a man from God, because he does not observe the Sabbath." (John

---

7. How was Jesus Christ rejected as a "living stone"?

9:16) Finally, the Jewish supreme court, the San-
hedrin, sentenced Jesus to death on the false
charge of blasphemy. (Matthew 26:63-66) With
a view to carrying out the penalty, the Jewish
rulers changed the charge against Jesus from
blasphemy to sedition. At their instigation, the
Roman governor, Pilate, ordered the execution
of him on a stake like the worst kind of political
criminal.—Luke 23:1-24.

[8] The action of men in rejecting Jesus Christ
as a foundation did not alter Jehovah God's own
estimation of his Son. Since the Most High fore-
ordained him as the one through whom the human race would be redeemed and as the "living
stone" on whom the Christian congregation would
be built, Jesus, as Peter states, was a "chosen"
one and continued to be such. There was never
any doubt in the mind of the Father about the
Son's carrying out the divine purpose without a
single flaw. Jehovah knew that his Son was perfect in devotion and affection. On earth, Jesus
Christ proved his deep love for his Father by
doing his Father's will perfectly while undergoing
great suffering. The Son's faithfulness under severe testing made him very precious in the eyes
of the Most High. So the Christian congregation
is blessed by having as its foundation the one
whom Jehovah God regards as his most highly
valued Son. (Ephesians 2:20-22) And devoted
members of this congregation strive hard to imitate the faithful course of Jesus Christ.

[9] Those to whom the apostle Peter wrote shared
God's view of his Son. As the apostle stated: "It
is to you, therefore, that he is precious, because

8. What is Jehovah's estimation of his Son?
9. Why could first-century believers be sure that their faith
would not come to disappointment?

you are believers." (1 Peter 2:7a) They recognized that Jesus Christ was the extremely valuable foundation cornerstone that the Father had laid in heavenly Zion, fulfilling the words of Psalm 118:22 and Isaiah 8:14; 28:16. Because of being in harmony with Jehovah's evaluation of his Son and putting their faith in him as the foundation cornerstone, first-century believers could rest assured that they would not experience disappointment, a shattering of their hopes. No one can damage the costly, precious foundation that is firmly established in the heavens and thus cause loss to those whose hopes are intimately bound up with it. As long as believers remained in union with Christ, the congregation's unshakable foundation, they were certain of receiving the object of their faith, namely, life without end. The unbelievers, however, would experience great loss. The apostle Peter continued:

> "But to those not believing, 'the identical stone that the builders rejected has become the head of the corner,' and 'a stone of stumbling and a rock-mass of offense.' These are stumbling because they are disobedient to the word. To this very end they were also appointed."—1 Peter 2:7b, 8.

[10] Because the prominent Jewish religious leaders refused to accept the Son of God as their ideal and to build their hopes for everlasting life on him, they lost out on the grand privilege of being Kingdom heirs. Jesus Christ had warned them: "The [repentant] tax collectors and the [repentant] harlots are going ahead of you into the kingdom of God." (Matthew 21:31) The course taken by those religious leaders did not prevent

---

10. How did Jesus Christ become "a stone of stumbling and a rock-mass of offense"?

Jesus from becoming "the head of the corner," the crowning stone of "a spiritual house." Moreover, in treating Jesus Christ as a stone that was unsuitable for their building work, these men were at the same time still forced to reckon with him as a stone that stood in their way. They could not ignore God's Son even after his death and resurrection, for his faithful disciples boldly continued witnessing about him. (Acts 5:28) Thus Jesus Christ became a rock over which all who persist in unbelief stumble to a calamitous fall. Just as those who show themselves to be genuine believers are appointed to salvation, so the ones who prove themselves to be unbelievers are appointed to experience loss. The Son of God even said with reference to himself: "Everyone falling upon that stone will be shattered. As for anyone upon whom it falls, it will pulverize him."—Luke 20:18.

RESULTS FROM 'COMING TO THE LIVING STONE'

[11] First-century believers, by accepting Jesus Christ as the divinely chosen, precious "living stone," came to be like "living stones." In what way? They ceased to be 'dead in trespasses and sins,' enjoying instead a "newness of life" as sons of God. (Romans 6:4; Colossians 2:13) Through Christ, the "living stone," life benefits were imparted to them. However, they were not to lie about as lifeless building stones and serve no useful purpose. No, they were to form a harmonious building. To form a unified structure, they needed to manifest the same kind of self-sacrificing love toward one another that their Exemplar had manifested toward them. (John 13:34) They were

11. How did first-century believers come to be like "living stones"?

also to be workers, as was Jesus Christ on earth. The Son of God was fully absorbed in doing his Father's will, responding to the needs of others and helping them to start on the way to everlasting life.—John 4:34.

[12] The words of the apostle Peter forcefully emphasize that Christians who are being built up by God into a spiritual house, a sanctuary or temple, have important work to do. (Compare 1 Corinthians 3:5-17; 6:19.) Note that Peter says: "You yourselves also as living stones are being built up a spiritual house for the purpose of a holy priesthood." Yes, this temple of "living stones" is also a "holy priesthood." Every spirit-begotten Christian, therefore, is a priest, serving loyally under the great High Priest Jesus Christ. Such a Christian does not need any man or a body of men to officiate for him in a priestly capacity. As a priest, his work is "to offer up spiritual sacrifices acceptable to God through Jesus Christ." (1 Peter 2:5) But what are these sacrifices?

[13] Peter says that they are "spiritual," hence not animal or grain offerings presented on some material altar. The time for making material sacrifices of this nature came to an end when the Son of God offered himself up as an acceptable sin-atoning sacrifice.—Hebrews 10:11, 12.

[14] Even in the Hebrew Scriptures we find indications as to the nature of acceptable "spiritual sacrifices," as in the following passages: "Offer thanksgiving as your sacrifice to God." (Psalm 50:14) "Let them offer the sacrifices of thanks-

12. Into what are the "living stones" built up, and so what is their responsibility?
13-15. What are the "spiritual sacrifices," and how can this be proved Scripturally?

giving and declare his works with a joyful cry."
(Psalm 107:22) "May my prayer be prepared as
incense before you, the raising up of my palms as
the evening grain offering." (Psalm 141:2) "We
will offer in return the young bulls of our lips."
(Hosea 14:2) Thus the "spiritual sacrifices" would
include such things as prayer, praise and thanksgiving.

¹⁵ The Christian Greek Scriptures provide us
with yet more detail. We are told: "Through him
[Christ] let us always offer to God a sacrifice of
praise, that is, the fruit of lips which make public
declaration to his name. Moreover, do not forget
the doing of good and the sharing of things with
others, for with such sacrifices God is well
pleased." (Hebrews 13:15, 16) In Philippians 2:17,
the apostle Paul speaks of "the sacrifice and public
service to which faith has led you," and upon
which he himself was "being poured out like a
drink offering." These passages emphasize the
importance of being actively concerned about the
spiritual and physical welfare of others, being
willing to expend time, energies and assets in
their behalf. Such a concern is manifest by sharing
God's message with fellow humans and coming
to the aid of persons in physical need, as did their
Exemplar, Jesus Christ. Think of it, the Most
High views what his servants do to promote the
welfare of their fellow humans as a pleasing
sacrifice of praise.

¹⁶ Because of the grand things that Jehovah
God had done for them through the Son, first-
century believers had good reason to feel com-
pelled "to offer up spiritual sacrifices." At one

16, 17. What sound reasons are there for offering such "spiritual
sacrifices" and declaring God's "excellencies"?

time they were in great "darkness" and without hope. While a part of the world, they were under the domination of its "ruler," Satan, the "authority of the darkness." (John 14:30; Colossians 1:13) The non-Jewish peoples were virtually in total ignorance respecting the true God and his purposes. They had no standing before him. The apostle Peter called attention to this fact when he said: "You were once not a people, but are now God's people; you were those who had not been shown mercy, but are now those who have been shown mercy." (1 Peter 2:10) Yes, by accepting Jesus Christ, both Jews and non-Jews became "a chosen race, a royal priesthood, a holy nation, a people for special possession." (1 Peter 2:9) They were "chosen" by God as his people, called to be king-priests in association with Jesus Christ, constituting a nation set aside for a holy or sacred purpose, and were obtained as the Most High's own property with the priceless blood of his Son. (Compare Exodus 19:5, 6; Revelation 5:9, 10.) What an outstanding display of mercy this was to the spiritual Israelites! Members of this "holy nation" enjoyed divine enlightenment and the light of divine favor. That contrasted sharply with the time when they were in "darkness," alienated from the Most High and ignorant of his will and purpose.

[17] In view of their being granted Jehovah's recognition and unmerited favor, these disciples of Jesus Christ were moved to declare to all what the Most High had done for them by means of his Son. They simply could not stop speaking to others about the "excellencies," the marvelous deeds, of their heavenly Father.

[18] Today all true disciples of Jesus Christ, including those of the "great crowd" who come into association with that "holy nation," should likewise feel impelled to live upright lives and to be active in helping others to gain divine approval. (Revelation 7:9-15) It should be our heart's desire to expend ourselves in efforts to aid persons who are in spiritual need. Our thus imitating the Son of God will do much to enrich our lives. What joy we can experience from contributing to the happiness, comfort and strengthening of our fellowmen! (Acts 20:35) In turn, we gain the affection and appreciation of those in whose behalf we unselfishly give of our time, energies and assets. While some may fail to show gratitude, we still have the deep inner satisfaction of having pleased our heavenly Father. And because of doing his will, we can rest assured of his aid and guidance. (1 John 3:22) May we continue reaping bountiful blessings from copying the example of the One who is most precious in the eyes of Jehovah God.

---

18. What application should we personally make of what we have considered in this chapter, and why?

6

Submission to Authority That Is Rewarding

THERE can be wisdom in submission, in show- ing subordination to existing arrangements. Whatever apparent appeal it might have, total independence is undesirable, unrealistic. No one person on earth can do everything or know every- thing. Just as we are dependent on air, sun, food and water for life, so, too, we need other persons and what they can do for us if we are to benefit from life and to enjoy it.

² Governmental arrangements, employer- employee relationships, family ties, association with the Christian congregation, our very living among people, all impose on us certain duties. We owe something in return for what we receive from others. Of primary importance in discharg- ing these responsibilities toward humans is our recognizing the position of Jehovah God. As the Creator, he rightly is the Supreme Sovereign to whom we owe all things. In a vision, the apostle John heard 24 elders declare: "You are worthy, Jehovah, even our God, to receive the glory and the honor and the power, because you created all things, and because of your will they existed and were created." (Revelation 4:11) Our making

---

1. Why can we say that submission to existing arrangements is wise and beneficial?
2. How should the fact of Jehovah's being the Supreme Sover- eign affect our life?

a similar acknowledgment of Jehovah as the Most High is not just a matter of words. In all our relationships, we can demonstrate that we are submissive to God's will for us and acknowledge Jesus Christ as our appointed Lord.

"FOR THE LORD'S SAKE"

³ The apostle Peter forcefully presented this elevated view of the major reason for subjection to human authority. He wrote: "For the Lord's sake subject yourselves to every human creation: whether to a king as being superior or to governors as being sent by him to inflict punishment on evildoers but to praise doers of good."—1 Peter 2:13, 14.

⁴ The 'human creations' to which we should be in subjection are the man-made ruling authorities. They are 'human creations' because men, not God, have created the positions of kings and lesser rulers or governors. The Most High has merely allowed such to come into existence and is tolerating them, as they do serve a useful purpose under the present conditions. Because governmental authorities exist by his permission, persons who rebel against them are revolting against the "arrangement of God," a provision that he has as yet not seen fit to end and replace by a heavenly kingdom through his Son. (Romans 13:1, 2) In the days of the apostle Peter, the Roman emperor or Caesar appointed governors to administer affairs in the imperial provinces, including Judea. These governors were directly responsible to the emperor in maintaining law and order in the territory under their jurisdiction. As they carried out their duties, the governors would "inflict

3, 4. What are the 'human creations' to which we should be in subjection, and why can they thus be identified?

punishment on evildoers"—robbers, kidnappers, thieves and seditionists. But they would also "praise doers of good," that is, honor upright persons by giving them public recognition as men of merit and by protecting their person, property and rights.

⁵ It is not primarily to escape punishment and to procure "praise" for themselves that Christians are urged to be in subjection. But it is "for the Lord's sake." This Lord is Jesus Christ, for the apostle Peter earlier identified him as such. (1 Peter 1:3) The Scriptures speak of the Son of God as "Lord over both the dead and the living." (Romans 14:9) He, therefore, occupies a position that no human ruler has ever held. As 'Lord over the dead,' Jesus Christ can summon them before him by restoring them to life. The scope of Jesus' lordship extends even beyond his having authority over living and dead humans. After his own resurrection, the Son of God said: "All authority has been given me in heaven and on the earth." (Matthew 28:18) Surely, it is wisdom on our part to submit ourselves to human rulers for the sake of One who has far, far greater authority than they do.

⁶ What is meant by subjecting ourselves to men in high governmental station "for the Lord's sake"? Our recognition of Jesus Christ as our Lord is to be the motivating force behind proper subjection to rulers. The Son of God set the perfect example in this regard. He did not revolt against the demands of the governmental authority nor did he teach others to do so. Rather, he

5. For whose sake should we be in subjection, and why is he rightly called "Lord"?
6, 7. How do we subject ourselves to human rulers "for the Lord's sake"?

urged: "If someone under authority impresses you into service for a mile, go with him two miles." (Matthew 5:41) 'Pay back Caesar's things to Caesar.'—Matthew 22:21.

[7] At times governments may order citizens to register for various purposes, or they may call upon them to support certain community building and farming projects, perhaps in connection with construction of roads, dams or schools. (Compare Luke 2:1-3.) In all these matters, Christian conscience is, of course, to be considered. However, where there is no issue involved that would offend one's Scripturally trained conscience, it can contribute to the advancement of the "good news" when the Christian does what he can to show himself both submissive and cooperative. It would be highly improper to agitate against any particular projects or to become outright rebellious toward governmental authority on any level. The Biblical injunction is to "be in subjection and [to] be obedient to governments and authorities as rulers, to be ready for every good work." A belligerent, arrogant stand does not harmonize with the teaching and example of God's Son.—Titus 3:1, 2.

"AS SLAVES OF GOD"

[8] Showing how proper submission to authority can serve to further the cause of true worship, the apostle Peter writes: "For so the will of God is, that by doing good you may muzzle the ignorant talk of the unreasonable men." (1 Peter 2:15) Christians, by doing what rulers regard as good, decent or law-abiding while, at the same time, preserving a good conscience before God,

---

8. What benefits can come from proper subjection to rulers?

may receive commendation. This results in silencing ignorant men who may falsely charge servants of the Most High with being stubborn, insubordinate, antisocial, seditious or subversive. The laudable conduct of Christians thus proves to be the very best defense against having their good name defamed.

⁹ But does a Christian's submission to rulers mean abject slavery to them, being *totally* subservient? The inspired answer is, No. The apostle Peter continues: "Be as free people, and yet holding your freedom, not as a blind for badness, but as slaves of God."—1 Peter 2:16.

¹⁰ As Christians, we have been set free from slavery to sin and death. (John 8:31-36) The Son of God has even emancipated us from the fear of a violent death, by means of which fear Satan the Devil has been able to keep men in slavery, maneuvering them, through the dictatorial orders of men, to act contrary to their own conscience. (Hebrews 2:14, 15) Because of being a free people, however, our conscience cannot be subservient to the dictates and threats of any man or group of men. Our submission to rulers is voluntary and is limited by the superior commands of the Supreme Sovereign, Jehovah God. We cannot become the abject slaves of any man, rendering unquestioning obedience without regard for divine law. As the apostle Peter pointed out, Christians are "slaves of God." Hence, we gladly submit to the wishes of the governmental authorities to the extent that there is no direct conflict with our worship of the Most High. Otherwise, we must

---

9, 10. Why is our subjection to governmental authority not like the subjection of a cringing slave to his master?

take the position voiced by Peter and the other apostles when before the Jewish supreme court: "We must obey God as ruler rather than men." —Acts 5:29.

A FREEDOM, WITH LIMITS

[11] However, it would be wrong for us to live as though political governments had no authority over us, defying them in matters that are not out of harmony with divine law. Such disrespectful conduct constitutes a misuse of Christian freedom. The freedom that we enjoy is bounded by our being slaves of God. It provides no license for casting off proper restraints, indulging in badness or treating with contempt laws that may inconvenience us but which are designed to protect life and the environment. Rather, we should show by our conduct that we appreciate the good purpose behind traffic laws, antipollution regulations, hunting and fishing restrictions and the like.

[12] Yes, we have *obligations* toward others. The nature of these duties is affected by the particular relationship that we have with Jehovah God and with our fellow humans. The apostle Peter points out these obligations and admonishes: "Honor men of all sorts, have love for the whole association of brothers, be in fear of God, have honor for the king."—1 Peter 2:17.

[13] All humans are the product of God's creation and bought with the precious blood of Jesus Christ.

---

11. What attitude toward governmental authority would constitute an abuse of Christian freedom?
12. What determines the kind of obligations that we have toward others?
13. (a) Why are all humans deserving of honor? (b) What do we owe our spiritual brothers? (c) What should determine the kind of honor that is given to humans? (d) What do we owe to God alone?

That is why we rightly honor them, treating them with respect and impartiality. (Acts 10:34, 35; 1 Timothy 2:5, 6) The whole "association of brothers," however, deserves far more than just the formal respect that is the due right of humans generally. To our brothers, we additionally owe deep love, affection. Moreover, while an earthly sovereign and lesser officials should be granted the honor for which their position calls, the Most High God alone is deserving of reverential, worshipful fear. Consequently, the honor that is given to any man must always be limited by a wholesome regard for Jehovah God and his commands. There is no objection, for example, to addressing rulers by their customary titles when these do not attribute to them the kind of honor that belongs to God alone. But mortal humans are not the saviors of Christians nor the ones through whom all blessings come. (Psalm 146:3, 4; Isaiah 33:22; Acts 4:12; Philippians 2:9-11) Hence, a genuine Christian does not address men in a way that calls into question his own fear of God and exalts rulers far above what their station requires.

ARE ALL OFFICIALS DESERVING OF HONOR?

[14] In view of the Biblical injunction to honor rulers, some persons may ask with reference to a certain official: 'How can I respect or honor someone who may be morally corrupt?' The point to keep in mind is that the moral standing of the official is not the basis for such honor. Rather, the authority that he represents and exercises

14, 15. (a) Why does the moral standing of a ruler or an official not affect whether the Christian will honor him? (b) What can we learn from the way in which the apostle Paul dealt with officials?

calls for a certain kind of respect. If there were no regard for duly constituted authority, anarchy would reign, with consequent damage to society, including Christians.

[15] The apostle Paul's dealings with officials illustrate that what rulers are as persons has no bearing on the type of honor that should be shown them. Ancient historian Tacitus described Roman Governor Felix as a man who "thought that he could do any evil act with impunity," and who, "indulging in every kind of barbarity and lust, exercised the power of a king in the spirit of a slave." Still, out of regard for the office that Felix occupied, Paul respectfully opened his defense before this man with the words: "Knowing well that this nation has had you as judge for many years, I readily speak in my defense the things about myself." (Acts 24:10) Despite the fact that King Herod Agrippa II lived in incest, Paul showed him due honor, saying: "I count myself happy that it is before you I am to make my defense this day, especially as you are expert on all the customs as well as the controversies among Jews." (Acts 26:2, 3) Although Governor Festus was a worshiper of idols, Paul still addressed him as "Your Excellency."—Acts 26:25.

PAYING TAXES

[16] Besides giving men the kind of honor that befits their authority, Christians are also under divine command to be conscientious about paying taxes. The Scriptures tell us: "Render to all their dues, to him who calls for the tax, the tax; to him who calls for the tribute, the tribute; to him

---

16. What counsel are Christians given at Romans 13:7?

who calls for fear [by reason of his authority, including the power of life and death], such fear; to him who calls for honor, such honor." (Romans 13:7) Why is it right to pay taxes and to be honest in reporting income?

[17] The ruling authorities render vital services to ensure the safety, security and welfare of their subjects. Included are the maintenance of roads, the provision of law-enforcement bodies, courts, schools, health services, postal systems and the like. For the services rendered, the government is entitled to compensation. Hence, Christians rightly view payment of taxes or tribute as the payment of a debt. Just how the ruling authorities will thereafter use the taxes received is not the responsibility of the Christian. Misuse of tax or tribute receipts on the part of officials does not entitle the Christian to refuse to pay his debt. Under the present arrangement of things, he needs governmental services and, therefore, in good conscience, pays what is required. When it comes to paying off a debt to an individual, that person's misuse of monies would not cancel one's debt. Similarly, regardless of what governments may do, the Christian is not relieved of his duty to pay taxes and tribute. He is to be exemplary in conforming to the legal requirements in reporting income or the purchase of items on which duty must be paid. His conscientiousness in these matters prevents the bringing of reproach on him and the Christian congregation. It also puts true worship in a favorable light, to the honor of God and Christ.

---

17. (a) Why should Christians view the payment of taxes the same as the payment of debts? (b) Why should Christians be exemplary in the payment of all taxes?

EMPLOYER-EMPLOYEE RELATIONSHIPS

[18] A Christian's relationship to governmental authority is not the only relationship that calls for proper subjection. At his place of work, for example, he may be accountable to a supervisor or a superior. Back in the first century C.E., when slavery was common in the Roman Empire, many Christians found themselves working as slaves or servants. Appropriately, God's Word discusses their obligations toward their masters. We today can apply the principles of conduct in the master-slave relationship to the employer-employee relationship.

[19] Directing his counsel to house servants or domestics, the apostle Peter wrote:

> "Let house servants be in subjection to their owners with all due fear, not only to the good and reasonable, but also to those hard to please. For if someone, because of conscience toward God, bears up under grievous things and suffers unjustly, this is an agreeable thing. For what merit is there in it if, when you are sinning and being slapped, you endure it? But if, when you are doing good and you suffer, you endure it, this is a thing agreeable with God."—1 Peter 2:18-20.

[20] What did heeding this counsel require? While discharging his responsibilities as a slave, the Christian was to manifest proper fear or regard for his master, not wanting to displease him. This fear was to be shown even if the master proved to be inconsiderate, harsh or unreasonable in his demands. The master may have been a man who

18. To what present circumstance can the Scriptural principles about the master-slave relationship be applied?
19. What counsel did Peter give to Christian house servants?
20. (a) How would a house servant be in subjection "with all due fear"? (b) What situations might have resulted in suffering for a Christian slave?

found fault even with work that was well done. He may have demanded that the Christian slave do things that were contrary to God's law. Because of faithfully obeying the dictates of his godly conscience, the Christian slave may have suffered unjustly for refusing to steal or to lie for his master. At other times, too, the slave may have been the object of physical and verbal abuse.

²¹ In harmony with Peter's counsel, the Christian slave would not rise up against his harsh master. He would continue to do his work conscientiously, and patiently bear up under mistreatment. This course would be agreeable in God's eyes, for it would not reflect unfavorably on Christianity. Others could see that true worship had exerted an influence for good on the slave. It could move them to investigate Christianity in order to find out how a mistreated slave could exercise such commendable self-control. By contrast, if a slave *wronged* his master and was severely disciplined for it, people would see no particular merit in his quietly taking punishment.

²² Today a Christian who faces a particularly trying situation at work may be able to procure other employment. But this may not always be possible. He may be working under a contract or be forced to continue laboring under undesirable conditions because other jobs simply are not available. So his situation may differ very little from that of a house servant in the first century C.E.

21. What good could result from a slave's patient endurance of mistreatment?
22. How would a Christian employee want to conduct himself at work?

who could not get away from an unreasonable master. Therefore, as long as a Christian continues in the employ of someone else, he would do his utmost to perform quality work, and patiently and uncomplainingly put up with any abuse to which he may be subjected and which could not be stopped by Scriptural means. He also would continue to treat his employer with due respect and consideration.

JESUS' EXAMPLE—AN ENCOURAGEMENT

²³ Clearly, it is never easy for anyone to have to endure injustice. Happily, however, we have a perfect model to follow, namely, our Lord Jesus Christ. His example can be a real source of encouragement. In consoling mistreated Christian slaves, the apostle Peter pointed to the example of Jesus, saying:

> "In fact, to this course you were called, because even Christ suffered for you, leaving you a model for you to follow his steps closely. He committed no sin, nor was deception found in his mouth. When he was being reviled, he did not go reviling in return. When he was suffering, he did not go threatening, but kept on committing himself to the one who judges righteously."—1 Peter 2:21-23.

²⁴ Thus the apostle reminded Christian slaves that one of the reasons for which they were called to be disciples of the Son of God was to demonstrate a spirit like his while subjected to unjust suffering. Especially on the final day of his life as a man on earth, Jesus Christ endured much. He was slapped, hit with fists, spit on, scourged with a whip (which was probably fitted with

23, 24. (a) Whose example can encourage us when we are subjected to mistreatment for doing what is right? (b) What did this one face, and how did he conduct himself?

pieces of lead or bone or barbs to tear the flesh), and, finally, nailed to a stake like a criminal of the worst kind. Yet, he submitted to all these indignities, never reviling or threatening the men responsible for meting out such unwarranted treatment. Jesus Christ knew that his life course had been pure, but he did not take matters into his own hands to vindicate himself. He committed his cause to the Father, confident that his God and Father would render a righteous judgment in his behalf. We, too, can be sure that the Almighty takes note of any injustices that we may experience. He will balance the scales of justice, provided we continue to bear up patiently under suffering. Surely, if the sinless Son of God was willing to endure mistreatment, we followers of his have even greater reason to do so, recognizing that we are sinful creatures.

²⁵ The suffering that Jesus Christ underwent was actually for our benefit, giving us additional motivation for imitating him. This aspect is stressed in the apostle Peter's further words:

> "He himself bore our sins in his own body upon the stake, in order that we might be done with sins and live to righteousness. And 'by his stripes you were healed.' For you were like sheep, going astray; but now you have returned to the shepherd and overseer of your souls."—1 Peter 2:24, 25.

²⁶ By reason of our being sinners, we are undeserving of the gift of life. The Bible tells us: "The wages sin pays is death." (Romans 6:23) Jesus Christ, however, willingly took upon himself the penalty for our sins, dying sacrificially like a

---

25. How have we benefited from Christ's suffering?
26, 27. What effect should Christ's suffering in our behalf have on us?

blameless, uncomplaining lamb in our behalf. Through his suffering the extreme penalty of a shameful death on a stake, the Son of God made it possible for believing humans to be set free from sin and to begin living a life of righteousness. Considering the suffering of Jesus Christ in our behalf, we should certainly be moved to show deep appreciation for what he has done for us. This requires that we imitate Jesus in all areas of life, including our being willing to undergo mistreatment for righteousness' sake, as he did. Whenever we are subjected to injustices, we do well to think about the suffering that our Lord experienced.

27 Such contemplation can impress on our minds the importance of conforming to Christ's example so that we do not miss the *purpose* of his great suffering for us. In our sinful state, we were in a pitiable condition, comparable to that of straying sheep without the guidance of a loving shepherd. This was so because, as sinners, we were alienated from our Great Shepherd, Jehovah God. However, on the basis of Jesus' sacrifice and our faith in it, a reconciliation has been effected. (Colossians 1:21-23) Hence, we have come under the loving care, protection and guidance of the overseer of our souls, namely, Jehovah God, and of his "chief shepherd," Jesus Christ. (1 Peter 5:2-4) Truly, then, no amount of affliction for righteousness' sake would be too great to bear in demonstrating our appreciation for what Jesus Christ has done. How far greater was Christ's suffering in our behalf than any mistreatment that we may undergo for his sake!

WORK ARRANGEMENTS WITH BELIEVERS

[28] Not all Christian slaves in the first century C.E., however, had unreasonable masters at whose hands they endured mistreatment. On account of the existing social conditions at that time, even some Christians had slaves. When the slave and his master were disciples of the Son of God, both men needed to look at their spiritual relationship in the correct light. Directing his admonition to slaves with believing owners, the apostle Paul stated: "Let those having believing owners not look down on them, because they are brothers. On the contrary, let them the more readily be slaves, because those receiving the benefit of their good service are believers and beloved."—1 Timothy 6:2.

[29] Why was this counsel needed? The believing slave was a joint heir with Christ and, therefore, enjoyed a spiritual equality with his believing master. Consequently, the slave needed to guard against reasoning that this spiritual equality annulled the secular relationship existing between them and the authority of the master in that relationship. Such an attitude could easily have led to a slave's taking advantage of his master, not doing his best in discharging his duties. The apostle Paul's counsel came to grips with any wrong conclusions that slaves may have drawn from their brotherly relationship with other members of the congregation. Because of being in such a relationship with their masters, they had even stronger reason to discharge their duties in a

28, 29. (a) What counsel did the apostle Paul give to Christian slaves with believing owners? (b) Why was such counsel needed?

fine way. It was their privilege to do something for a Christian brother, and this should have been a source of great joy to them.

[30] Similarly today, if a Christian works under the direction of a believing supervisor or is in the employ of a believer, he should want to do his very best. It is his brother who is getting the benefits from his labor. If he were to do poor quality work or to be self-sparing, he would be a disappointment and a source of irritation to this brother. (Proverbs 10:26) What lack of affection he would be showing for the brother whom he is under obligation to love!—1 John 4:11.

[31] On the other hand, Christian masters or employers were not to disregard the fact that they, too, had a master, Christ. The realization of their being accountable to the Son of God was to affect the way in which they treated their slaves or workers. Commenting on this, the apostle Paul wrote: "You masters, keep dealing out what is righteous and what is fair to your slaves, knowing that you also have a Master in heaven."—Colossians 4:1.

[32] Furthermore, if Christian brothers are laboring or rendering services for us in the capacity of doctors, lawyers, electricians, carpenters, plumbers, repairmen and the like, we certainly would want to give them just compensation. Would it not be inappropriate to take advantage of our spiritual relationship by postponing payment to a Christian brother while using a large part of our earnings for lavish entertainment, luxuries or ex-

---

30. Why should a Christian today do his best if he is working under the supervision of a believer?
31. What counsel did Christian masters have to keep in mind?
32. What responsibility do we have toward believers who may be laboring or rendering services for us?

pensive vacations? In business matters, should we not want our fellow believers to get whatever they are entitled to receive? It is certainly fine when we can thereby aid our brothers to make a living. If special consideration is shown us, we rightly regard this with appreciation, recognizing that our fellow believers are not obligated to give us special rates or to favor us over others. In all these matters, then, we can show that we want to do all things in a way pleasing to our heavenly Head, God's Son.

WIFELY SUBJECTION

[33] Marriage is still another relationship that calls for submission to a head. Therefore, Peter links his discussion of wifely subjection with his previous admonition about subjection under adverse conditions by starting out with the Greek word meaning "in like manner." We read:

> "In like manner, you wives, be in subjection to your own husbands, in order that, if any are not obedient to the word, they may be won without a word through the conduct of their wives, because of having been eyewitnesses of your chaste conduct together with deep respect."—1 Peter 3:1, 2.

[34] The circumstance under which Christian wives are here encouraged to be in subjection is an unfavorable one. When a husband does not accept the principles of God's Word, he may make life very difficult for a Christian wife, being harsh and unreasonable in dealing with her. But this does not excuse her from acting in harmony with the fact that a husband is the head of the

---

33. (a) What admonition is given to Christian wives? (b) In 1 Peter 3:1, what is significant about the word meaning "in like manner"?
34. Under what circumstance is the apostle Peter encouraging a wife to be in subjection, and why may this not be easy?

family. So, whenever his requests do not conflict with divine law, a Christian wife would want to do her utmost to please her husband.

[35] As the apostle Peter pointed out, her fine example may help the husband to become a believer. A wife's thus gaining her husband "without a word," however, does not mean that she would never share Scriptural thoughts with him, but she would let her commendable actions speak even louder than words. A husband would then be able to see that the conduct of his wife is chaste or pure in speech and action and that she has deep respect for him.

[36] What the apostle Paul wrote about women provides still more details as to what may be expected from a Christian wife. In his letter to Titus, he stated:

"Let the aged women be reverent in behavior, not slanderous, neither enslaved to a lot of wine, teachers of what is good; that they may recall the young women to their senses to love their husbands, to love their children, to be sound in mind, chaste, workers at home, good, subjecting themselves to their own husbands, so that the word of God may not be spoken of abusively."—Titus 2:3-5.

[37] According to this admonition, a woman should conscientiously seek to conduct herself in a manner revealing her appreciation of the fact that her whole life course comes under the view of Jehovah God and of the Lord Jesus Christ. She will work hard to use her tongue to build up and encourage others, not resorting to slander or hurtful gossip. Moderation in food and drink are certainly in order. As a wife and mother, the Chris-

---

35. How might a wife gain her husband "without a word"?
36, 37. According to Titus 2:3-5, to what should a Christian woman give attention in order to be an exemplary wife?

tian woman is to be exemplary in her love, seeing to it that she is doing her part in providing nourishing meals and making the home a clean and pleasant place. Love for her husband and her children includes her being willing to put the family's interests ahead of her own. A husband should not be able to find evidence that his wife is seriously neglecting her duties. But he should be able to see that, when compared with unbelieving women, she is indeed exemplary.

BALANCED VIEW OF ADORNMENT

[38] Important, too, is a wife's keeping adornment in the right perspective. The apostle Peter stressed that a Christian wife is not to put the main emphasis on making herself attractive by means of showy adornment. He said: "Do not let your adornment be that of the external braiding of the hair and of the putting on of gold ornaments or the wearing of outer garments." (1 Peter 3:3) In the first century C.E., women spent much time and effort in braiding their long hair into elaborate, attention-getting designs, including harps, trumpets, wreaths and crowns. Additionally, they adorned themselves with very ornate apparel and an abundance of gold chains, rings and bracelets. For a Christian woman, such extreme attention to physical adornment was inappropriate, as it would suggest that her main object in life was her own person rather than her being pleasing to Jehovah God and the Lord Jesus Christ. Moreover, women who live mainly for show or fashion are often the victims of pride, envy, and status seeking, which rob the mind and heart of a spirit of calmness and produce frustration and irritability.

---

38. What counsel about adornment do we find at 1 Peter 3:3, and how should it be understood?

[39] However, this does not mean that a Christian wife would give little attention to her appearance. When similarly counseling against showy dress, the apostle Paul also said: "I desire the women to adorn themselves in well-arranged dress, with modesty and soundness of mind." (1 Timothy 2:9) So a Christian wife does well to watch that she does not present an unsightly appearance to her husband by being careless about her dress, grooming and physical appearance. Furthermore, the Bible states that "the woman is man's glory." (1 Corinthians 11:7) Clearly, a lazy, unkempt woman is no credit or glory to her husband. She degrades his appearance in the eyes of others. And if the husband takes reasonable pride in his own appearance, by sloppiness his wife could be a source of much irritation. Hence, it is most desirable that a Christian woman's dress and adornment indicate that she has good judgment in choosing what is modest, or decent, and becoming to her person.

"THE QUIET AND MILD SPIRIT"

[40] Nevertheless, a Christian wife's real beauty lies in what she is at heart. The apostle Peter wisely urged that her adornment "be the secret person of the heart in the incorruptible apparel of the quiet and mild spirit, which is of great value in the eyes of God." (1 Peter 3:4) This "quiet and mild spirit" is not to be confused with a veneer of outward sweetness. For example, a woman may be soft spoken and meekly submit, in

---

39. Why should a wife not neglect her appearance?
40. (a) What makes a Christian woman truly beautiful? (b) With what should "the quiet and mild spirit" not be confused?

word, to the wishes of the family head. Yet, she might, at heart, try to dominate her husband by being rebellious, plotting and scheming.

⁴¹ In the case of the woman who genuinely possesses "the quiet and mild spirit," this humble spirit is a reflection of her true inner self. How can a woman determine whether this "spirit" is part of her permanent adornment? She might ask herself: 'What happens when my husband, on occasion, is inconsiderate, unreasonable or shirks his responsibility? Do I often flare up, become enraged and harshly censure him for his failings? Or, do I usually strive to remain calm inside myself and avoid open confrontation?' A woman with a "quiet and mild spirit" is not just seemingly peaceful on the surface but like an active volcano inside herself, ready to erupt. No, under trying circumstances, she seeks to maintain a calm and even temperament both outwardly and inwardly, causing observers to be deeply impressed by the inner strength she shows and the kind way in which she handles herself.

⁴² Such a "quiet and mild spirit" distinguished God-fearing women of pre-Christian times. Calling attention to this fact, the apostle Peter wrote:

"For so, too, formerly the holy women who were hoping in God used to adorn themselves, subjecting themselves to their own husbands, as Sarah used to obey Abraham, calling him 'lord.' And you have become her children, provided you keep on doing good and not fearing any cause for terror."—1 Peter 3:5, 6.

41. How might a woman determine whether "the quiet and mild spirit" is part of her permanent adornment?
42. According to 1 Peter 3:5, 6, who did have a "quiet and mild spirit"?

⁴³ As one of the "holy women" of pre-Christian times, Sarah placed her hope and confidence in Jehovah. Unlike Lot's wife who longingly looked back at Sodom, only to perish, Sarah willingly left the comforts of Ur and continued to dwell with her husband, Abraham, in tents for the rest of her life. Along with Abraham, she looked forward to a permanent abiding place under divine rulership. (Hebrews 11:8-12) Sarah certainly did not attach too much importance to material possessions and comforts. She lived in a manner that revealed a spiritual outlook. Sarah appreciated that God would richly reward her at the time of the resurrection. Similarly, Christian women today wisely make pleasing Jehovah God their main objective in life.—Compare Proverbs 31:30.

⁴⁴ The beautiful Sarah had deep respect for her husband. When unexpected visitors arrived, Abraham felt no hesitancy in saying to his faithful companion: "Hurry! Get three seah measures [.6 bushel; 22 liters] of fine flour, knead the dough and make round cakes." (Genesis 18:6) That very day Sarah referred to Abraham as her "lord." Since she did so inside herself and not in the hearing of others, this clearly shows that she was, at heart, submissive to her husband.—Genesis 18:12.

⁴⁵ However, Sarah was not a woman of weak personality. When she noted that Ishmael, the son of the Egyptian slave girl Hagar, was "poking fun" at her own son Isaac, Sarah spoke out strongly to Abraham, saying: "Drive out this slave girl

---

43. What shows that Sarah was a 'holy woman' who hoped in God?
44. What proves that Sarah had deep respect for her husband?
45. What shows that Sarah did not have a weak personality?

and her son, for the son of this slave girl is not going to be an heir with my son, with Isaac!" But that she was making a forceful appeal to Abraham, not improperly demanding or commanding, is shown by Jehovah's approval of Sarah's request. The Almighty noted the appeal made in the right spirit, and directed Abraham to carry it out.—Genesis 21:9-12.

⁴⁶ Likewise, a submissive Christian woman need not be spineless or wishy-washy. She may express definite personal views and take the initiative in handling certain affairs that are of importance to the family's happiness. But she would endeavor to have in mind her husband's wishes and feelings, letting these guide her when making purchases, decorating the home or caring for other household business. If she is uncertain about his view on a particular activity or major purchase, she can avoid problems through prior consultation. By seeking to discharge her wifely duties in a way that is pleasing to God, she will also please her husband, not giving him any valid reason to find fault. Such a wife usually gains a position of honor and dignity in the family. Her situation proves to be like that of the capable wife described at Proverbs 31:11, 28: "In her the heart of her owner has put trust . . . Her sons have risen up and proceeded to pronounce her happy; her owner rises up, and he praises her." A husband who is confident that his wife will act wisely and not endanger the welfare of the family would feel no need to lay down numerous rules designed to control unwise actions. There will simply be a fine

---

46, 47. (a) How can a woman who expresses strong views and takes initiative demonstrate that she is submissive? (b) What should we expect from a God-fearing woman?

understanding between them. In caring for family affairs, she will enjoy using her capabilities and initiative to the full.

⁴⁷ To be a God-fearing woman in the Biblical sense, a Christian wife needs to be industrious and able to take the initiative in helping others. So she will not be a woman who lives virtually 'in the shadow' of her husband. (Compare Proverbs 31: 13-22, 24, 27.) This is evident from the description of Christian women who qualified to be put on a special list in the first century C.E. We read: "Let a widow be put on the list who has become not less than sixty years old, a wife of one husband, having a witness borne to her for fine works, if she reared children, if she entertained strangers, if she washed the feet of holy ones, if she relieved those in tribulation, if she diligently followed every good work." (1 Timothy 5:9, 10) Note that her record of fine works would go back to the time when she was "a wife of one husband." So, we do not want to confuse a "quiet and mild spirit" with what may actually be only a lack of initiative and industriousness.

BENEFITS FROM SHOWING A CHRISTLIKE SPIRIT

⁴⁸ Since Christ is 'a model for all his disciples to follow,' a Christian wife will want to apply herself in becoming more like him when faced with unfavorable circumstances. (1 Peter 2:21) This requires that she be honest with herself in evaluating her words and actions. Then, by prayerfully considering the example of Jesus Christ and continuing to ask Jehovah God for the help of his spirit in becoming a better wife, she will come

---

48. How can a Christian wife become more like the Son of God?

to have the "mind of Christ" to a greater degree. (1 Corinthians 2:16) Her advancement will become apparent to others. This is so because the more we think about the fine qualities and praiseworthy acts of someone whom we love, the more we will want to be like that one.

⁴⁹ Even when a husband is inconsiderate, unreasonable or shirks responsibility, a wife can have every confidence that applying Bible principles will get the best results possible under the circumstances. Little is gained by a wife who makes a big issue over every wrong decision that her husband has made, thus disregarding Scriptural counsel to be submissive. Humans are prone to defend themselves even when they are wrong. So, if a wife makes a 'major case' whenever her husband uses poor judgment, she may get a reaction that is opposite to what she is seeking. He may become more determined to ignore what she says in order to prove to her that he does not need her advice. On the other hand, if her reaction reflects an understanding of the fact that we sinful humans cannot altogether avoid mistakes in judgment, he may be far more inclined to give consideration to her thoughts the next time. He will find it easier to keep his pride from becoming too intimately involved in the matter.

⁵⁰ By encouraging her husband in a kind, gentle manner, a Christian wife may cause him to think seriously about the way he is handling himself and then to start making changes in his life. While progress may be slow, a wife does gain an im-

---

49-51. (a) Why is it always wise for a wife to apply Bible principles? (b) What fine benefits can result from faithful adherence to the Scriptures? (c) What "cause for terror" should a Christian woman not fear, and why?

mediate reward. What is it? She avoids the tremendous emotional stress, bitterness and unpleasantness to which open confrontation with her husband would lead.—Proverbs 14:29, 30.

[51] A wife's faithful adherence to the Scriptures in conduct and speech may not always cause her unbelieving husband to become a Christian. But she still has the satisfaction of knowing that her course is 'well-pleasing to God.' The commendable way in which she handles her responsibilities as a wife and mother is part of her record of fine works that is like a treasure deposited in heaven. That treasure will yield rich dividends in the form of divine blessings. (Matthew 6:20) Appreciating the importance of maintaining a good standing with God, she should "keep on doing good" and not fear any "cause for terror"—any abuse, threats or opposition that may result because of her being a disciple of Jesus Christ. Instead of yielding to fear and forfeiting her relationship with Jehovah and his Son, she may view her experience as suffering for the sake of Christ. Thus she proves herself to be a daughter of submissive Sarah, a godly woman of faith.

"ACCORDING TO KNOWLEDGE"

[52] Just as a wife has certain duties because of her relationship with a husband, so does a husband because of his relationship with a wife. The apostle Peter reminded husbands of this, using the Greek word for "likewise" or "in like manner" to link his admonition to them with his previous counsel to wives, saying:

---

52. What is significant about Peter's use of the Greek word meaning "likewise" or "in like manner" when counseling Christian husbands?

"You husbands, continue dwelling *in like manner* with them according to knowledge, assigning them honor as to a weaker vessel, the feminine one, since you are also heirs with them of the undeserved favor of life, in order for your prayers not to be hindered."—1 Peter 3:7.

[53] It is noteworthy that the inspired apostle, himself a married man, first calls attention to the fact that the manner in which a husband dwells or lives with his wife is to be governed by "knowledge." (Mark 1:30; 1 Corinthians 9:5) Surely a husband would want to know his wife well—her feelings, strengths, limitations, likes and dislikes. But, even more importantly, he should come to know what his responsibilities are as a Christian husband. By really knowing his wife and also knowing his own God-assigned role, a husband can 'continue dwelling with his wife according to knowledge.'

[54] The Scriptures show that the husband is the head of his wife. But he is not an absolute head, for he is required to submit to the headship of Jesus Christ in handling family affairs. "The head of every man is the Christ," the Bible tells us. (1 Corinthians 11:3) "Husbands," wrote the apostle Paul, "continue loving your wives, just as the Christ also loved the congregation and delivered up himself for it." (Ephesians 5:25) Thus, the way in which the Son of God treats the Christian congregation serves as a model for husbands in discharging their family obligations. There certainly is nothing tyrannical or cruel about Jesus Christ's exercise of headship over the congregation. He even gave up his life for it.

---

53. What should govern the manner in which a husband dwells with his wife?
54. What does the exercise of headship require?

Therefore, a husband's headship does not entitle
him to dominate his wife, putting her in a low,
degraded position. Instead, it places on him the
responsibility of being self-sacrificing in his love,
being willing to put his wife's welfare and interests
ahead of his personal desires and preferences.

⁵⁵ Since Jesus Christ is the perfect example for
them, husbands do well to acquaint themselves
with what he did in dealing with his disciples.
More importantly, husbands should strive to conform to the pattern of the Son of God in discharging their family responsibilities. Consider
just a few of the many things that Jesus Christ
did while on earth in caring for his disciples.

⁵⁶ The Son of God was genuinely interested in
the spiritual welfare of his followers. Even when
they were slow to grasp vital matters, he did not
become impatient with them. He took time to
make things clear for them and saw to it that
they really understood his teaching. (Matthew
16:6-12; John 16:16-30) When they continued to
have a problem in having an appreciative view of
their relationship to one another, Jesus repeated
points on the need for humbly ministering to
others. (Mark 9:33-37; 10:42-44; Luke 22:24-27)
On his final night with them he fortified his teaching on humility by washing their feet, thus setting
the example for them. (John 13:5-15) Jesus also
took into consideration the limitations of his
disciples and did not give them more information
than they could comprehend at the time.—John
16:4, 12.

55. Since Jesus Christ is the example, what should Christian
husbands do?
56, 57. (a) How did the Son of God show genuine interest in
the spiritual welfare of his disciples? (b) In view of Jesus'
example, what might a husband ask himself?

[57] A Christian husband might, therefore, ask himself: 'How concerned am I about the spiritual welfare of my wife and children? Do I make sure that they really understand Bible principles? When noting wrong attitudes and actions, do I make it clear just *why* such are wrong and *why* changes should be made? Do I take into consideration their limitations and watch that I do not require too much?'

[58] The Son of God was also alert to take note of what his disciples needed from a physical standpoint. When the apostles returned to Jesus from a preaching tour and made report of their activity, he said: "Come, you yourselves, privately into a lonely place and rest up a bit." (Mark 6:31) Similarly, a husband wisely sees to it that his wife and children have time for relaxation and refreshment from the regular routine of life.

[59] In exercising headship, Jesus Christ does not hem in the members of the congregation by a list of involved regulations. He gave them the really important commands and guidelines as a basis for their reaching proper decisions in handling the problems of life. His self-sacrificing love, coupled with his confidence and trust in the disciples, in effect, "compels" them to respond with like love, doing their utmost to please him.—2 Corinthians 5:14, 15; compare 1 Timothy 1:12; 1 John 5:2, 3.

[60] In a similar way, a husband's showing confidence in his wife can do much to preserve a happy marriage. A wife who has little latitude to

58. How might a husband imitate Jesus' example in considering the physical needs of his family?
59, 60. (a) How has Jesus Christ shown confidence and trust in his disciples? (b) How can this help a husband in exercising headship?

use initiative in caring for her responsibilities will soon lose joy in her work. She will feel stifled in using her knowledge, talents and abilities, resulting in frustration. On the other hand, when her husband entrusts certain important matters to her good judgment, she will have pleasure in handling things in a way that will delight her husband.

"ASSIGNING THEM HONOR AS TO A WEAKER VESSEL"

[61] In dwelling with a wife according to his knowledge of her as a person and of his Scriptural responsibilities toward her, a husband would also be assigning her "honor as to a weaker vessel, the feminine one." Because a woman's bodily makeup imposes more physical limitations on her than is usually true of men, she is the "weaker vessel." But she is to occupy an honorable or dignified standing in the family. The following words of the apostle Paul illustrate how a husband can assign honor to his wife: "In this way husbands ought to be loving their wives as their own bodies. He who loves his wife loves himself, for no man ever hated his own flesh; but he feeds and cherishes it, as the Christ also does the congregation."
—Ephesians 5:28, 29.

[62] Husbands generally do not downgrade their own accomplishments, make themselves appear incompetent, subject their bodies to cruel treatment, and disregard their need for rest and refreshment. They do not want to have the reputa-

---

61-63. (a) What do the Scriptures say about the way in which a husband should deal with his wife? (b) What things would a husband avoid if he indeed assigns an honorable place to his wife? (c) When it comes to important family matters, what should a husband be willing to do? (d) Why is it not enough to take into consideration merely the spoken word when making final decisions?

tion of being "good-for-nothings," but desire a dignified standing in the eyes of others. If a husband is really a Christian, he will not make light of whatever weaknesses his wife may have, belittle her or otherwise make her feel low and degraded. He would accord his wife the same kind of dignity and consideration that he wants for himself, making her feel wanted, appreciated and needed.

[63] For a wife to have an *honorable* position in the home, her husband needs to be willing to discuss family matters with her in a calm and reasonable way, getting her thoughts and ideas. The wife should be able to express herself freely, with the assurance that what she says in discussing serious matters will not be lightly dismissed but be given due consideration by her husband. (Compare Judges 13:21-23; 1 Samuel 25:23-34; Proverbs 1:5, 6, 8, 9.) Furthermore, a husband needs to be alert to take note of more than just the spoken word. Deep inner feelings can be revealed by the tone of voice, facial expressions or by lack of enthusiasm or spontaneity. (Compare Proverbs 15:13.) A husband who has come to know his wife will not ignore such things and blindly go ahead with something that might give rise to needless irritation.

[64] Of course, as head of the family, when a husband is thoroughly satisfied in his own mind that the interests of the family as a whole would be injured thereby, he would not give in to his wife's desires. (Compare Numbers 30:6-8.) He recognizes that he is Scripturally obligated to uphold what he honestly believes is right, despite any

64. When would a husband not give in to his wife, and why is this beneficial?

emotional displays by his wife. For the husband to comply with his wife's wishes against his better judgment would mean dishonoring God, who has entrusted the man with the position of family head. And if matters thereafter led to hardships for the family, this could embitter him toward his wife. On the other hand, his remaining firm for what he definitely believes to be the right course will benefit the family. If his decision is made prayerfully and in harmony with Scriptural principles, his wife may well come to see the wisdom of the decision made and be glad that her husband remained firm. This should enhance her respect for him and contribute to her happiness and that of the whole family.

A SPIRITUAL REASON

[65] There is a compelling reason for a Christian husband to live with his believing wife "according to knowledge," granting honor to her. It is not just the benefit of increased peace in the family. The Christian apostle Peter showed to his fellow believers an even greater reason. He pointed out that husbands are 'heirs with their wives of the undeserved favor of life.' By reason of his sacrificial death, Jesus Christ opened up to both men and women the opportunity of being relieved from the condemnation of sin and death, with eternal life in view. Hence, a wife can have just as much of an approved standing before God and Christ as does her husband. There is serious reason then for a husband to exercise care that he does not treat his wife as if she were an inferior person having less value in God's eyes than he does.

---

65. What spiritual reason is there for a Christian husband to live with his believing wife "according to knowledge"?

⁶⁶ When marital affairs are not handled according to the example of Jesus Christ with his congregation, this has a damaging effect on the spiritual state of both husband and wife. Yes, 'prayers could be hindered.' In a home where there is a readiness to quarrel, to take offense, to harbor grudges and to act with harshness and unreasonableness, it is difficult to appeal to God in prayer. Because of feeling condemned at heart, a person would not have freeness of speech. (1 John 3:21) Then, too, Jehovah God has set forth requirements for hearing prayers. He will not listen to appeals for aid from persons who are merciless, unwilling to forgive the trespasses of others. (Matthew 18:21-35) Only those who strive to harmonize their lives with his commands are given a favorable hearing. (1 John 3:22) Neither husbands nor wives who fail to imitate in their marriage the example of Jesus Christ with his congregation can expect to have divine assistance in dealing with their problems. On the other hand, faithful obedience to Scriptural admonition guarantees divine approval and blessing. Surely, this is a fine reward that comes from submitting to the headship of God's Son.

SUBMISSION IN THE CHRISTIAN CONGREGATION

⁶⁷ Within the Christian congregation, there is also real need for recognition of Christ's headship. This recognition will affect the attitude and conduct of the individual members toward one another. According to Jesus' own words, his congregation was to be a brotherhood. He said to his

---

66. When marital affairs are not handled Scripturally, why does serious spiritual harm result?
67. According to Matthew 23:8-11, what attitude should exist within the Christian congregation?

disciples: "You, do not you be called Rabbi, for one is your teacher, whereas all you are brothers. Moreover, do not call anyone your father on earth, for one is your Father, the heavenly One. Neither be called 'leaders,' for your Leader is one, the Christ. But the greatest one among you must be your minister [servant, *Kingdom Interlinear Translation*]."—Matthew 23:8-11.

[68] No one, therefore, is to play the prince in the congregation. But those who serve as elders and teachers in it are to imitate the Master, Christ, in humbly slaving for their brothers. However, since the congregation is a brotherhood composed of both young and old, male and female, individual members of the congregation are not free to take liberties that would violate the natural sense of propriety. The apostle Paul counseled Timothy: "Do not severely criticize an older man. To the contrary, entreat him as a father, younger men as brothers, older women as mothers, younger women as sisters with all chasteness."—1 Timothy 5:1, 2.

[69] At the time the apostle wrote these words, Timothy was likely in his thirties. Although serving as an appointed elder, he was being admonished to keep in mind that he was still comparatively young. If an older man needed correction, Timothy was not to be harsh with him but was to appeal to him with the respectful bearing of a son standing before his father. (Compare the respectful way in which Jacob was entreated by his sons, as recorded at Genesis 43:2-10.) Older women, too, were to be shown the consideration and

---

68, 69. (a) Since the congregation is a brotherhood, what liberties should not be taken? (b) What did Timothy have to keep in mind when dealing with members of the congregation?

kindness that were due a mother. Not even with young men could Timothy take liberties, but he was to deal with them as he would with beloved fleshly brothers. Because of the strong attraction men feel toward the opposite sex, it was most appropriate that Timothy be cautioned to treat young women as his own fleshly "sisters with all chasteness." This meant that, in his association with young Christian women, he was to remain chaste, pure or clean in his thoughts, words and actions.

70 In our relationship with other members of the congregation, we need a spirit of humility in order to keep our place and not violate the natural sense of decency and propriety. Rightly, then, the apostle Peter admonished: "You younger men, be in subjection to the older men." (1 Peter 5:5) Young men should strive to cooperate with older men, especially the appointed elders of the congregation. It would surely be inappropriate for a young man to speak to older men or act toward them in a way that would be unthinkable if he were dealing with his own fleshly father. But what may a young man do to maintain a spirit of submissiveness? He may find it beneficial to think about the commendable qualities of older brothers and their record of faithful service. This can contribute toward deepening his love and appreciation for them.—Compare Hebrews 13:7, 17.

71 Of course, Peter did more than encourage just the young men to be submissive to the older men. He continued: "All of you gird yourselves

70. (a) Why is a spirit of submissiveness needed in order to maintain proper conduct in the congregation? (b) What can help one in maintaining a submissive spirit?
71. What is meant by our 'girding ourselves with lowliness of mind'?

with lowliness of mind toward one another." The original-language expression for "gird yourselves with lowliness of mind" carries the thought of tying such lowliness of mind on oneself with knots. That "lowliness of mind" was to be like an apron or a garment girded on by a slave. Hence, the spirit that Peter encouraged is one of willingness to serve and benefit others. How fine it is when we treat all in the congregation with respect and deference, according them the dignity that they deserve! This course leads to Jehovah's blessing and favor, for Peter adds: "God opposes the haughty ones, but he gives undeserved kindness to the humble ones."—1 Peter 5:5.

[72] Truly, our showing the kind of submission that harmonizes with the Holy Scriptures pays a rich reward. It will never worsen a bad situation but will give us a good conscience before God and men. Subjection to governmental authorities, employers, supervisors or an unbelieving husband can provide a fine witness respecting the value of true Christianity and may help others to become disciples of God's Son, with eternal life in view. In our own case, we can rest assured that Jehovah God will richly reward us for having followed the course that is pleasing in his sight. Yes, proper subjection to authority is a vital part of our enjoying the best way of life now.

---

72. What rewards come from showing proper subjection?

7

Aliens and Temporary Residents of Exemplary Conduct

A PERSON who stands out as being very different from the people of the community in which he lives is often viewed with distrust and suspicion. His conduct may come under closer scrutiny than that of persons native to the area. Sadly, some individuals may become prejudiced against a whole race, nationality or tribe because of the misconduct of a single foreigner in their neighborhood. Even governments make laws and regulations that apply only to aliens. If a foreigner's conduct is regarded as undesirable, he may be deported.

² Why is all of this of serious concern to the Christian? How should it affect his or her way of life?

³ In this world, true Christians are "aliens and temporary residents," for they are looking forward to a permanent abiding place as part of the "new heavens and a new earth" of God's making. (1 Peter 2:11; 2 Peter 3:13) Because genuine disciples of Jesus Christ strive to think and act in harmony with the Holy Scriptures, unbelievers, or

---

1, 2. How are aliens often viewed, and why?
3. (a) Why are true Christians "foreigners" in this world? (b) How do unbelievers view them, and why?

those who make only a pretense of practicing Christianity, may look down on them as if they were undesirable "foreigners." But the world's view of a Christian should not cause him to feel ashamed. From the divine standpoint, his alien status is one of dignity. Therefore, the Christian will want to do his utmost to conduct himself in a way that does not give anyone valid reason for reproaching him.

⁴ Writing to fellow believers, the apostle Peter called attention to their honorable standing as "aliens and temporary residents." At the outset of his first letter, we read:

> "Peter, an apostle of Jesus Christ, to the temporary residents scattered about in Pontus, Galatia, Cappadocia, Asia, and Bithynia, to the ones chosen according to the foreknowledge of God the Father, with sanctification by the spirit, for the purpose of their being obedient and sprinkled with the blood of Jesus Christ."—1 Peter 1:1, 2.

⁵ Back in the first century C.E., believers found themselves scattered in various locations and living in the midst of a large non-Christian population. Often they were unjustly despised by their neighbors. So it must have been encouraging for them to read or to hear Jehovah's estimation of them as set forth in Peter's letter. They were actually God's 'chosen ones,' the elect. The Most High had made them his possession, his people. Long before the Christian congregation composed of Jews and non-Jews came into existence, the Almighty foreknew that there would eventually be such a group of his servants scattered in various parts of the earth. Through the operation of

4, 5. (a) In the first century C.E., why could the apostle Peter speak of Christians as "temporary residents scattered about"? (b) How did Jehovah God view them?

God's spirit on them, they were sanctified or set apart for sacred use. The objective of Jehovah's dealings with them was that they might be his obedient children, doing his will. Their knowledge of this use of them by the Universal Sovereign should surely have stirred them deeply, moving them to want to live up to the noble purpose to which God assigned them.

⁶ Of course, it was not because of their own merit that believers came to be a chosen, sanctified people. As individuals, they were sinners and had to be cleansed, and so the apostle Peter referred to them as 'being sprinkled with the blood of Jesus Christ.' This reminds us of the cleansing procedure for an Israelite who became ceremonially defiled by, among other things, touching a human corpse. To be clean again, the individual had to be sprinkled with the water of cleansing. (Numbers 19:1-22) Similarly, the atoning benefits of Christ's sacrifice had been applied to Christians, enabling them to have a clean conscience before God and to have freedom of speech in approaching him in prayer. (Hebrews 9:13, 14; 10:19-22) Then, too, when the Israelites were taken into a covenant relationship with Jehovah, Moses sprinkled the people with the blood of sacrificial victims. (Exodus 24:3-8) Hence, the words about 'being sprinkled with the blood of Jesus Christ' may also call attention to the fact that these believers had been taken into the new covenant mediated through Jesus Christ and made valid by his shed blood and that they now shared in this covenant's benefits.

6. (a) How did Christians gain their clean standing before God? (b) What may be included in their 'being sprinkled with the blood of Jesus Christ'?

⁷ Like believers of the first century C.E., devoted disciples of Jesus Christ today have an honorable standing before Jehovah God. In this world they must conduct themselves as *exemplary* "aliens" and "temporary residents." Otherwise, they bring reproach on Jehovah God and the congregation of his people. All, therefore, need to take to heart the apostle Peter's admonition: "Beloved, I exhort you as aliens and temporary residents to keep abstaining from fleshly desires, which are the very ones that carry on a conflict against the soul."—1 Peter 2:11.

⁸ Because of being "aliens and temporary residents" in this passing system of things, we cannot afford to allow ourselves to become unduly attached to anything within the now-existing human framework. No earthly ties, sorrows, joys or possessions are permanent. Time and unforeseen occurrence befall all people and can change one's circumstances suddenly and dramatically. (Ecclesiastes 9:11) Hence, there is real wisdom in heeding the apostle Paul's counsel: "Let those who have wives be as though they had none, and also those who weep be as those who do not weep, and those who rejoice as those who do not rejoice, and those who buy as those not possessing, and those making use of the world as those not using it to the full; for the scene of this world is changing." (1 Corinthians 7:29-31) For us to be completely absorbed in sorrows or joys that are the product of these ever-changing circumstances and relationships could work against our drawing closer to the Most High and his Son, with serious loss to ourselves.

7. What does our "alien" status require from us?
8. To what should we not allow ourselves to become unduly attached, and why?

⁹ The situation of the majority of mankind demonstrates clearly why we should not try to 'make use of the world to the full.' People generally either are not aware of God's promise of "new heavens and a new earth" or have no real faith in such a coming righteous new order. So they have nothing but their present life on which to focus attention. They lack a solid hope regarding the future. That is why they are so wrapped up in thinking about their daily needs and are intent on gaining as much from the world as possible. (Matthew 6:31, 32) Their eyes light up at the prospect of getting fine clothing, sparkling jewels, expensive ornamentation, beautiful furniture or luxurious homes. They may hope and seek to impress others by means of material possessions. —1 John 2:15-17.

¹⁰ The Christian, by contrast, recognizes that an eternal future lies before him. It would be foolish for him to become so absorbed in the affairs of life that he has virtually no time for the Creator on whom his future depends. This does not mean that true servants of God cannot properly enjoy many of the fine things that money can buy. But even wholesome pleasures and beneficial material possessions must never become the focal point of our life, not if we really see ourselves as "temporary residents" in this present system. While not being wasteful or careless with our assets, we rightly regard them much as do trustworthy persons who merely rent a furnished apartment, tools, equipment or other items that they may need. Such persons care for these well but never become

9, 10. (a) What accounts for the way in which worldlings regard possessions? (b) Why should our view of possessions be different from that of unbelievers?

completely attached to them as if they were permanent possessions. Our life should show that we recognize that nothing in the present system gives any guarantee of permanence, that we are but "aliens" and "temporary residents," moving forward toward the promised new order of God's making.

'ABSTAIN FROM FLESHLY DESIRES'

[11] However, to make a success of our way of life as Christians, far more is required of us than just a realization that, as far as our life now in this world is concerned, our circumstances are subject to unforeseeable change. We also need to give serious attention to the Bible's exhortation to 'abstain from fleshly desires.' These are the wrong cravings or desires in the body members of the individual. The apostle Paul's letter to the Galatians reveals what sins these wrong cravings incite. After showing that the person who is led by God's spirit does not carry out "any fleshly desire," the apostle enumerates the works of the flesh—"fornication, uncleanness, loose conduct, idolatry, practice of spiritism, enmities, strife, jealousy, fits of anger, contentions, divisions, sects, envies, drunken bouts, revelries, and things like these."—Galatians 5:16, 19-21.

[12] As a result of inherited sin, we are subject to strong pressures to become involved in the works of the flesh, to 'carry out fleshly desires.' The unwholesome cravings are like an invading army that is seeking to gain the mastery over the whole soul, the whole person, causing him to give in to

11. What would be included in the fleshly desires from which we must abstain?
12, 13. (a) How do fleshly desires "carry on a conflict against the soul"? (b) What must we do to maintain a clean standing before God?

the indulging of sinful passions. The Christian apostle Paul was very much aware of the struggle that can thus come about within the individual. With reference to his own case, he wrote: "I know that in me, that is, in my flesh, there dwells nothing good; for ability to wish is present with me, but ability to work out what is fine is not present. For the good that I wish I do not do, but the bad that I do not wish is what I practice." (Romans 7:18, 19) This conflict made it necessary for Paul to 'pummel his body and lead it as a slave, that, after he had preached to others, he might not become disapproved somehow.'—1 Corinthians 9:27.

[18] Similarly, our desire to maintain a clean standing before God and to receive his blessing will motivate us to exert ourselves so that any wrong cravings are kept under control. Why should we make a hard struggle harder through involvement with entertainment, reading matter, associations and circumstances that are bound to excite and build up the pressure of our sinful inclinations? More importantly, we need to take positive steps to protect ourselves. It is good to keep in mind that we cannot succeed in our own strength but need the encouragement of our devoted brothers and the help of God's spirit. The apostle Paul urged Timothy to "pursue righteousness, faith, love, peace, along with those who call upon the Lord out of a clean heart." (2 Timothy 2:22) If this is what we are doing, then, with the aid of the holy spirit, we can succeed in preventing wrong desires from gaining the mastery over us. Thus, our resisting fleshly desires by keeping our minds fixed on what is true, righteous, chaste, lovable, virtuous and praiseworthy will prevent

our becoming divinely disapproved. (Philippians 4:8, 9) After having sought to help others to succeed, we will not ourselves become failures.

FINE CONDUCT MAY HELP OTHERS TO ACCEPT TRUE WORSHIP

¹⁴ Our "abstaining from fleshly desires" is accompanied by still another very desirable benefit. The apostle Peter wrote: "Maintain your conduct fine among the nations, that, in the thing in which they are speaking against you as evildoers, they may as a result of your fine works of which they are eyewitnesses glorify God in the day for his inspection."—1 Peter 2:12.

¹⁵ In the first century, Christians were often the object of misrepresentation, depicted as "evildoers." Typical were accusations such as the following: "These men are disturbing our city very much, . . . and they are publishing customs that it is not lawful for us to take up or practice, seeing we are Romans." (Acts 16:20, 21) 'These men have overturned the inhabited earth.' 'They act in opposition to the decrees of Caesar, saying there is another king, Jesus.' (Acts 17:6, 7) The apostle Paul was accused of being "a pestilent fellow and stirring up seditions among all the Jews throughout the inhabited earth." (Acts 24:5) Leading men among the Jews in Rome told Paul: "Truly as regards this sect it is known to us that everywhere it is spoken against."—Acts 28:22.

¹⁶ The best defense against such misrepresentation is fine conduct. When Christians prove them-

---

14. How may others benefit by seeing us 'abstain from fleshly desires'?
15. In what way were Christians misrepresented in the first century C.E.?
16. (a) What is the true Christians' best defense against misrepresentation? (b) How can this help opposers?

selves to be law-abiding, faithfully pay their taxes, manifest willingness to perform any "good work," and in their personal occupations are diligent workers, honest in their dealings, and demonstrate real concern for the welfare of their fellow humans—the accusations made against them are shown up as false. (Titus 2:2–3:2) Even persons who repeat slanderous information about Christians could thus be helped to see the wrongness of their course and be moved to adopt true worship. Then, at the time of God's judgment inspection, such former misrepresenters of Christians may be numbered among those who glorify or praise the Most High.

[17] The fact that a Christian's living an upright life can be a tremendous force for good should cause us to think seriously about the way in which we treat others and the extent to which we are showing interest in our neighbors. Certainly we do not want to close our eyes to the needs of people next door. Of course, our being kind, obliging and polite neighbors is not just "good policy." It is *basic* to our being Christians. In his Sermon on the Mount, Jesus Christ admonished: "All things . . . that you want men to do to you, you also must likewise do to them." (Matthew 7:12) The Scriptures urge us: "As long as we have time favorable for it, let us work what is good toward all, but especially toward those related to us in the faith." (Galatians 6:10) "If possible, as far as it depends upon you, be peaceable with all men." (Romans 12:18) "Always pursue what is good toward one another and to all others."—1 Thessalonians 5:15.

---

17. In view of the wholesome effect of good conduct on observers, to what should we give serious consideration?

¹⁸ Clearly, being a Christian includes more than carrying out such vital requirements as attending meetings with fellow believers and sharing Bible truth with others. (Matthew 28:19, 20; Hebrews 10:24, 25) We are also under command to imitate the Son of God in our attitudes and actions, in what we are as persons, individuals. The apostle Peter wrote: "Finally, all of you be like-minded, showing fellow feeling, having brotherly affection, tenderly compassionate, humble in mind." (1 Peter 3:8) To be "like-minded," we need to "be fitly united in the same mind and in the same line of thought." (1 Corinthians 1:10) Our thinking should especially harmonize with that of Jesus Christ who expressed his love by surrendering his life for us. (John 13:34, 35; 15:12, 13) While true disciples of Jesus Christ are "like-minded," as is evident from their love and unity world wide, the questions that we individually must answer are: 'Am I genuinely contributing to this spirit of oneness and affection? How, and to what extent?'

¹⁹ If we truly love our spiritual brothers, we will be kind and forgiving. After a problem is discussed and a solution agreed upon, we will not continue to harbor grudges and deliberately shun certain members of the Christian congregation who may have contributed toward creating the difficulty. In harmony with Peter's counsel, we need to guard against falling victim to the callousness, the harshness and the pride that are common in the world. Others should be able to see that we have "fellow feeling" or are sympathetic toward those who are suffering, that we have warm love or affection for our spiritual brothers,

---

18, 19. In harmony with 1 Peter 3:8, what should be true of our attitudes and actions as Christians?

that we are "tenderly compassionate" or inclined to show pity, and that we do not have an exalted opinion of ourselves but are "humble in mind," willing to serve others.—Compare Matthew 18: 21-35; 1 Thessalonians 2:7-12; 5:14.

[20] Moreover, we are not to limit our expressions of sympathy, compassion and kindness just to fellow believers. (Luke 6:27-36) The apostle Peter went on to urge Christians not to 'pay back injury for injury or reviling for reviling, but, to the contrary, to bestow a blessing.' (1 Peter 3:9) This does not mean that we will praise persons who injure and revile us or shower them with affection. But we will accomplish the most good and have the greatest peace of mind and happiness if we continue to be kind and considerate in our dealings with them, hoping that they might change their ways and become recipients of divine blessings.

REASONS FOR NOT RETALIATING

[21] The fact that Jehovah God has mercifully forgiven us our sins on the basis of Jesus' sacrifice should move us to treat even our enemies in a kind, compassionate manner. Jesus Christ said: "If you do not forgive men their trespasses, neither will your Father forgive your trespasses." (Matthew 6:15) Hence, our inheriting permanent blessings from God is affected by our willingness to bless others. Jehovah God permits us to experience unkind treatment. Among the reasons for this is that we might have the opportunity to demonstrate that we are forgiving and compassionate toward our fellow humans. The apostle Peter expressed

20. What does heeding the counsel of 1 Peter 3:9 require of us?
21. How can Jehovah's example aid us in not retaliating?

this thought by going on to say: "You were called to this course [of blessing those who seek to injure you], so that you might inherit a blessing." (1 Peter 3:9) This is not to say that our heavenly Father wants others to injure us. He has simply not stepped in to prevent our being subjected to the problems of sinful humans living in a sinful world. And this lets us demonstrate whether we *really* want to be like him—kind, compassionate and forgiving.

²² Continuing his encouragement not to retaliate in word or in deed, Peter quotes from Psalm 34:12-16 and writes:

"For, 'he that would love life and see good days, let him restrain his tongue from what is bad and his lips from speaking deception, but let him turn away from what is bad and do what is good; let him seek peace and pursue it. For the eyes of Jehovah are upon the righteous ones, and his ears are toward their supplication; but the face of Jehovah is against those doing bad things.' "—1 Peter 3:10-12.

²³ These words of Peter emphasize that treating all persons in a kind manner is really the only proper way to live, the best way to live. The person who 'loves life,' appreciating it as a gift from God, and who wants to see "good days"—days that give him a sense of purpose and meaning in living —shows this by promoting the happiness of his fellow humans. He keeps his tongue in check, not using it to downgrade, revile, deceive or to defraud others. His desire is to shun all badness and to do what is good from God's standpoint. As a person

22. What encouragement does Psalm 34:12-16 provide about avoiding a vengeful spirit?
23, 24. (a) What does it mean for us to "love life" and to want to "see good days"? (b) How do we benefit by showing a love for life?

who seeks and pursues peace, he will not be aggressive or belligerent but will exert himself to promote good relations with and among others. —Romans 14:19.

²⁴ The person who demonstrates his love for life by helping others to enjoy happiness and peace makes himself a desirable associate. Others show by their words and actions that they view him as needed, wanted and appreciated. As a result, his life will never be empty or meaningless.—Proverbs 11:17, 25.

²⁵ Although his kindness may not always be received with gratitude, such a person is assured of Jehovah God's loving care. Since the eyes of the Most High watch over the righteous and his ears are always ready to hear them, he knows just what their needs are and may quickly respond to fill these. He will indeed cause them to "see good days," for the godly devotion they show "holds promise of the life now and that which is to come." (1 Timothy 4:8) On the other hand, those who practice what is bad—who do not work for the peace and happiness of others—can expect no expression of divine approval. God's "face" is against them with adverse judgment, for nothing escapes his notice.

A COURSE OF GAIN

²⁶ Keeping ever before us the benefits that result from fine conduct will help us to resist pressures to become involved in the world's degraded practices. The apostle Peter gives us powerful encouragement to this end, saying:

---

25. Why can we be certain of God's loving care and help?
26. According to Peter's words, who may wish to see us return to the corrupt practices of the world?

"The time that has passed by is sufficient for you to have worked out the will of the nations when you proceeded in deeds of loose conduct, lusts, excesses with wine, revelries, drinking matches, and illegal idolatries. Because you do not continue running with them in this course to the same low sink of debauchery, they are puzzled and go on speaking abusively of you. But these people will render an account to the one ready to judge those living and those dead. In fact, for this purpose the good news was declared also to the dead, that they might be judged as to the flesh from the standpoint of men but might live as to the spirit from the standpoint of God."—1 Peter 4:3-6.

²⁷ The time that a Christian may have spent in satisfying his sinful passions and desires while he was ignorant of God's will and purpose certainly should have been enough for him never to want to return to a life characterized by excesses and lack of moral restraint. We never want to forget how empty and meaningless a life of self-indulgence is, and the shame that goes along with it. (Romans 6:21) The vulgar, obscene entertainment, lewd dancing, and wild, passion-arousing music, which have become so prominent in the world, should repel, not attract, us. While it may not be easy to be spoken of abusively by former associates because we shun such things, we surely have nothing to gain by joining them in their wild parties and their unbridled way of life. But we do have much to lose by adopting worldliness. All practicers of what is bad must render an account for their actions before Jesus Christ, the one whom Jehovah God has appointed to judge the living and the dead. (2 Timothy 4:1) Because this judgment is certain, the "good news"

---

27. Why should we never want to return to the world's corruption?

was declared to the "dead," that is, to the spiritually dead who needed to repent, turn around and come to life from God's standpoint by having the atoning benefits of Christ's sacrifice applied to them.

[28] Those who do repent are indeed precious in Jehovah God's eyes, and he wants them to enjoy an eternity of happy living. Men of this world, however, do not recognize the fine standing that true Christians have with the Creator. Such worldlings look upon Christ's disciples as they do other men and judge them "as to the flesh," by the outward appearance. However, the fact that their judgment of us is an unfavorable one should not disturb us. What really counts is whether Jehovah God regards us as 'living as to the spirit,' that is, living spiritual lives. This will be the case if our life continues to be in harmony with the commands of the Most High.

[29] We do indeed have good reason to maintain fine conduct as "aliens and temporary residents" in this present system. The Most High commands it. His own example of kind, merciful dealing with us requires that we be considerate, compassionate and forgiving in our dealings with others. Our laudable conduct reflects favorably on our God and may aid others to become his servants. Only by maintaining fine conduct will we continue to experience Jehovah's blessing and finally receive eternal life in a permanent abiding place. No other way of life is so beneficial now and holds such grand promise for the future.

---

28. (a) Why might Christians "be judged as to the flesh from the standpoint of men"? (b) Why should such judgment not disturb us?
29. What good reasons do we have for maintaining fine conduct?

8

Help for Bearing Up Under Suffering

AT SOME time in our lives, we may need help with our problems, even desperately. If a series of tragedies were to befall us in quick succession, we could easily find ourselves sinking into hopeless despair. The burden might well seem more than we could bear. How good it is to have help at such a time!

² Our being disciples of Jehovah God's Son does not exempt us from needing aid. We are not immune to afflictions. The common lot of humankind continues to include sickness, accidents, floods, earthquakes, storms, crime, injustice and oppression. We should not expect the Supreme Sovereign to use his power to manipulate hereditary factors and environment so that we, as his servants, become uniquely free from any suffering due to these things. God's time for undoing all the hurtful effects of human sin is yet future. If he now caused his people to lead 'charmed lives,' we would doubtless see huge numbers flocking to serve him—for purely selfish reasons, not due to love and faith.—Compare John 6:10-15, 26, 27.

³ Not only will we inevitably experience distress from unpleasant conditions, but, because we *are* God's servants, we may also face persecution—

1, 2. Why can disciples of Jesus Christ not escape suffering?
3, 4. What suffering may true Christians experience that others do not undergo, and what questions may this bring?

perhaps from relatives, from neighbors or acquaintances, or from governmental authorities. Jesus Christ went so far as to say: "People will deliver you up to tribulation and will kill you, and you will be objects of hatred by all the nations on account of my name." (Matthew 24:9) The facts show that this has happened, right in the 20th century.

⁴ Why does the Almighty God permit his servants to undergo various trials? Since their way of life does not guarantee them freedom from common afflictions and since pursuing that way can even make them "objects of hatred," a person may wonder how such a way of life could truly be the best. Are there benefits that compensate for, yes, outweigh the afflictions? Can there actually be greater happiness in enduring some trial than in avoiding it? What will help us to succeed in bearing up under severe pressures? The answers to these questions can greatly aid and strengthen us.

WHO BEARS THE REAL RESPONSIBILITY?

⁵ It is vital that we never forget that our heavenly Father is not the source of suffering. He did not introduce sin into the world. A spirit son of God chose to rebel against his Maker, thus making himself Satan, a *resister* of the Most High. On account of his influence, the first human pair, Adam and Eve, deliberately violated divine law, bringing the judgment of death on themselves. (Genesis 3:1-19; John 8:44) Because Adam ruined his perfection, all his offspring were born in sin, subject to sickness, infirmity, old age and death.

5. What do we need to recognize about the source of suffering?

(Romans 5:12) As born sinners, we all fall short of being the kind of person we would like to be and ought to be. By our words and actions, we may unintentionally hurt others, adding to their afflictions. So we need to remember that God is not to blame for the difficulties produced by our own imperfections or those of our fellow humans. If his law had been obeyed, sickness, infirmity, old age and the many other causes of suffering would never have come into existence.

⁶ Then, too, our heavenly Father does not approve of man's inhumanity to man. The Bible says: "To trample underfoot any prisoner in the land, to deprive a man of his rights in defiance of the Most High, to pervert justice in the courts—such things the Lord has never approved." (Lamentations 3:34-36, *The New English Bible*) Those who mistreat fellow humans, in violation of God's law, will have to render an account to him. "Vengeance is mine; I will repay, says Jehovah." (Romans 12:19) Consequently, we need to exercise care that we do not become embittered toward our heavenly Father because of the suffering that results when men willfully and rebelliously disregard divine law.

⁷ Of course, Jehovah God has the ability to prevent Satan, the demons, wicked men and human sinfulness from causing all kinds of trialsome situations. However, since he does permit distressing circumstances to beset even his servants, this must be for good reasons.

---

6. How does Jehovah feel about man's inhumanity to man?
7. Since Jehovah God has permitted situations to develop that result in suffering for us, what must we conclude about his reasons for doing so?

FOR THE BENEFIT OF "VESSELS OF MERCY"

[8] The Scriptures explain that God's purpose in not taking action immediately against those responsible for bringing great suffering on others is for the ultimate benefit of righteously disposed ones. In his letter to the Romans, the Christian apostle Paul wrote:

"Is there injustice with God? Never may that become so! For he says to Moses: 'I will have mercy upon whomever I do have mercy, and I will show compassion to whomever I do show compassion.' So, then, it depends, not upon the one wishing nor upon the one running, but upon God, who has mercy. For the Scripture says to Pharaoh: 'For this very cause I have let you remain, that in connection with you I may show my power, and that my name may be declared in all the earth.' So, then, upon whom he wishes he has mercy, but whom he wishes he lets become obstinate.

"You will therefore say to me: 'Why does he yet find fault? For who has withstood his express will?' O man, who, then, really are you to be answering back to God? Shall the thing molded say to him that molded it, 'Why did you make me this way?' What? Does not the potter have authority over the clay to make from the same lump one vessel for an honorable use, another for a dishonorable use? If, now, God, although having the will to demonstrate his wrath and to make his power known, tolerated with much long-suffering vessels of wrath made fit for destruction, in order that he might make known the riches of his glory upon vessels of mercy, which he prepared beforehand for glory, namely, us, whom he called not only from among Jews but also from among nations, what of it?" —Romans 9:14-24.

[9] What Jehovah God may cause or may allow to develop in the lives of people can reveal just

8. What reasons are presented in Romans 9:14-24 as to why Jehovah God does not act immediately against those who cause others to suffer?
9. How did Pharaoh reveal himself to be a 'vessel of wrath'?

what kind of "vessels" they are. The Pharaoh on whom Jehovah, through Moses and Aaron, served notice for the release of the enslaved Israelites continued to harden himself against the Most High. As one plague after another came upon the Egyptians, this Pharaoh became more stubborn in his refusal to let the Israelites leave Egypt as a free people. Thus he revealed himself to be a 'vessel of wrath,' meriting destruction for rebellious defiance against the authority of the Supreme Sovereign, Jehovah God. At the same time, the cruel, unjust treatment given to the Israelites amply demonstrated that they were deservedly in need of mercy, pity or compassion.

[10] Note, too, that the apostle Paul called attention to the fact that God's name was involved in Jehovah's allowing Pharaoh to continue in stubborn defiance. If this haughty ruler had been destroyed immediately, there would not have been the opportunity for Jehovah God's power to be made known in such an extensive and diversified way, humiliating the many deities of the Egyptians and the magic-practicing priests. The ten plagues, climaxed by the destruction of Pharaoh and his military forces in the Red Sea, were such an impressive display of divine power that for years thereafter the surrounding nations were still talking about it. Thus the name of Jehovah came to be declared throughout the earth, bringing glory and honor to that name, and moving honesthearted ones to recognize his supreme position. —Joshua 2:10, 11; 1 Samuel 4:8.

---

10. By allowing Pharaoh to maintain his defiant course for a time, how did Jehovah make a great name for himself?

[11] Surely, the Israelites, as "vessels of mercy," benefited from what the Most High had done. His permission of oppression and then bringing it to an end in a magnificent demonstration of power helped them to know him better, providing them with a glimpse of his greatness that could not have been gained otherwise. Though painful, Israel's experience in Egypt certainly should have helped them to see the importance of having faith in his saving power, as well as having a wholesome fear of God. This was essential if they were to continue pursuing a way of life that would lead to happiness, security, peace and good health.—Deuteronomy 6:1-24; 28:1-68.

[12] Just as the inclination of people's hearts became manifest in that time, so the testing and trials that may befall us by God's permission can reveal whether our service to him is rightly motivated. It is the contention of God's adversary, Satan, that those who do the divine will are basically selfish. Respecting faithful Job, the adversary declared: "Everything that a man has he will give in behalf of his soul. For a change, thrust out your hand, please, and touch as far as his bone and his flesh and see whether he will not curse you to your very face." (Job 2:4, 5) By faithful endurance under suffering, we share in proving Satan's contention to be a lie and share in vindicating the good name of our heavenly Father, who trusts his loyal servants. What if Jehovah were to allow Satan, by means of his agents, to subject true Christians to very cruel

---

11. How did the Israelites benefit from their experience with Pharaoh?
12. As illustrated in the case of Job, what does Jehovah's permission of suffering enable us to do?

treatment that ended in death or crippling infirmity? What if some were even sexually assaulted or abused in other vile ways? These things are shocking. Yet there is nothing beyond the power of our heavenly Father to rectify fully in his due time. So, in some cases, he may see fit to let the trial be pushed to such an extreme point. Through faithfulness, even to the point of death, God's servants are thus given the opportunity to show beyond denial the genuineness of their devotion.

[13] Surprising as it may seem to some, the trials to which we may be submitted, whether from natural causes or from persecution, can nevertheless bring improvement in us *in a personal way*. The apostle Peter called attention to this. After pointing out that Christians are "safeguarded by God's power" so that their final salvation might be secured, the apostle states:

> "In this fact you are greatly rejoicing, though for a little while at present, if it must be, you have been grieved by various trials, in order that the tested quality of your faith, of much greater value than gold that perishes despite its being proved by fire, may be found a cause for praise and glory and honor at the revelation of Jesus Christ."—1 Peter 1:5-7.

[14] As Peter acknowledges, the suffering that we may experience is by no means pleasant. We can be actually "grieved" or pained by trials. Yet we can, at the same time, rejoice. Why? In part, the joy comes from recognizing that there is a spiritual benefit to be gained from successfully bearing up under affliction. What is that spiritual benefit?

13. What do the words of 1 Peter 1:5-7 reveal about the suffering to which Christians may be submitted?
14. Why can Christians rejoice when they are "grieved" by trials?

THE WAY SUFFERING CAN REFINE FAITH

¹⁵ The apostle Peter likened the effects that trials can have on a Christian's faith to the refining of gold by fire. The refining process removes the dross, leaving behind the pure gold. The highly increased value of the gold certainly makes the refining process worth while. Still, as Peter said, even gold tested by fire is perishable. It can wear away or be destroyed by other means. But not so with tried or tested faith. Genuine faith cannot be destroyed.

¹⁶ If we are to gain divine approval, it is absolutely essential that we have such faith. The Bible tells us: "Without faith it is impossible to please [God] well." (Hebrews 11:6) Truly, faith that is proved genuine under test greatly exceeds the value of refined gold. Our eternal future depends on such faith.

¹⁷ But how can trials refine faith so that it "may be found a cause for praise and glory and honor at the revelation of Jesus Christ"? This can happen in a variety of ways.

¹⁸ If our faith is strong, it will comfort and support us during a time of hardship. Then, having passed one trial successfully, we are strengthened to meet any further test. The experience will have demonstrated what our faith can do for us.

¹⁹ On the other hand, a particular trial may show up personality flaws, perhaps pride, stubbornness, impatience, worldliness or a love of ease and plea-

---

15. What effect can trials have on faith?
16. Why is it highly beneficial for us to have genuine faith?
17. What question might be raised about the effect of trials on faith?
18. How might faith reveal itself under trial, and how can this strengthen us?
19. What might a particular trial manifest as to weaknesses in faith, and how can this help us?

sure. Such traits are really born of weaknesses in faith. How so? In that they reveal that a person is not fully submitting himself to God's guidance and will regarding him. He is not convinced that his Father really knows best what will lead to happiness, and that following divine direction will always result in blessing. (Hebrews 3:12, 13) When trials expose weaknesses, the Christian can be alerted to the need to strengthen his faith in order to remain an approved servant of the Most High.

20 Therefore, if a particular situation shows up a defect in our faith, we can examine ourselves and determine what corrective measures to take. A person does well to ask: 'Why is my faith weak? Do I neglect study and meditation on God's Word? Do I take full advantage of opportunities to assemble with fellow believers in order to be strengthened by their expressions of faith? Do I tend to rely more on myself than I should, instead of committing all my cares and anxieties to Jehovah God? Are prayers, *heartfelt* prayers, really a daily part of my life?' Once the areas are established where improvement is needed, we need to put forth diligent effort to make changes in our routine of life, with a view to strengthening our faith.

21 By looking to God for guidance and patiently trusting in him to show us the way to relief from our trials, we can let these trying experiences aid us to become better servants of his. Then our faith will indeed "be found a cause for praise and glory and honor at the revelation of Jesus Christ." The

---

20. When trials expose weaknesses in our faith, what should we do?
21. What is meant by our faith's being "found a cause for praise and glory and honor at the revelation of Jesus Christ"?

Son of God will "praise," laud or commend our faith. By reason of our faith, he will richly reward us, thus bestowing "glory" on us. Before Jehovah God and the angels, he will "honor" us as his disciples. (Compare Matthew 10:32; Luke 12:8; 18:8.) This will mean our having before us an endless future of happy living. But what can we do while undergoing severe suffering to keep our faith from weakening?

HOW TO REACT UNDER STRONG PRESSURE

²² One thing that can help us to endure difficult trials successfully is to recognize their temporary nature. The refining of gold has a beginning and an end. So, too, any affliction we undergo will not continue indefinitely. If we keep near to our hearts God's promise of eternal life without sickness, outcry or pain, then even the worst of suffering in this system of things can be seen as being but "momentary and light." (2 Corinthians 4:17) Look forward to the time when surely "former things will not be called to mind, neither will they come up into the heart." (Isaiah 65:17) How grand to know those hard experiences will then not even be a painful memory!

²³ Then, too, our undergoing great suffering at the hands of men is rarely a daily experience. Our fine conduct actually gives little reason for anyone to harm us. It being the job of governmental authorities to maintain law and order, they may well praise Jehovah's servants for being law-abiding. In modern times, even opposers have been forced to make an acknowledgment similar

---

22. Our recognizing what fact about the length of trials can help us to endure?
23. Why would suffering not usually come on us for fine conduct?

to that made by the enemies of God's faithful
prophet Daniel: "We shall find in this Daniel no
pretext at all, except we have to find it against
him in the law of his God." Yes, Daniel was "trustworthy and no negligence or corrupt thing at all
was found in him." (Daniel 6:4, 5) The fact that
fine conduct in itself usually would not be the
reason for a Christian's being the object of hos-
tility may be why the apostle Peter raised the
following question: "Indeed, who is the man that
will harm you if you become zealous for what is
good?"—1 Peter 3:13.

²⁴ By his question, however, the apostle may
have instead been asking: 'Who can do *real* harm
to the upright Christian?' No man can inflict last-
ing injury on us. Jesus Christ told his disciples:
"Do not become fearful of those who kill the
body but cannot kill the soul; but rather be in
fear of him that can destroy both soul and body
in Gehenna." (Matthew 10:28) Yes, men can go
to the point of killing us, but they cannot take
away our right to be living souls. The Most High
God, by means of his Son, can and will restore his
faithful servants to life. It is Jehovah alone who
can destroy our title to life as living beings for all
eternity, consigning us to unending death with no
hope of a resurrection.

²⁵ Because of these truths, the apostle Peter
could say to his Christian brothers: "Even if you
should suffer for the sake of righteousness, you
are happy. However, the object of their fear do
not you fear, neither become agitated."—1 Peter
3:14.

---

24. Why can humans not inflict permanent injury on us?
25, 26. (a) Why can we be happy when suffering for the sake
of righteousness? (b) Why should we not fear the object of
our persecutors' fear?

[26] If we suffer "for the sake of righteousness," we can be happy because we have a clean conscience before God and men. We suffer for the right reason. A deep inward satisfaction and peace result from doing what we know to be pleasing to the Most High. However, as the apostle noted, to do this successfully depends on not giving way to fear. The apostle may here refer to the fear persecutors can inspire by their bringing affliction on God's people. Or, it could be the fear that the persecutors themselves have. For instance, because of not having faith that Jehovah God, through Christ, will resurrect the dead, the opponents of true Christians fear a threatened premature death. (Hebrews 2:14, 15) We servants of God, though, do not need to fear what unbelievers fear, as we have been freed from the fear of such a death and know that our heavenly Father will never forsake us. Therefore, we should not become "agitated," as by rising up in anger against our persecutors.

[27] What if we were to be brought before governmental authorities and questioned in a harsh, belittling manner? We would never want to retaliate in kind. Our confidence that God is backing us up may give us boldness, but it gives no excuse for belligerence or arrogance. (Compare Acts 4:5-20.) The apostle's counsel is: "Sanctify the Christ as Lord in your hearts, always ready to make a defense before everyone that demands of you a reason for the hope in you, but doing so together with a mild temper and deep respect." (1 Peter 3:15) If we failed to heed this advice and allowed ourselves to express contempt and disrespect, we would cease to suffer for the sake of righteousness.

27, 28. How can the counsel of 1 Peter 3:15 help us when brought before governmental officials and questioned in a harsh, belittling manner?

The governmental authority would feel justified in acting against us for disrespectful insubordination. Worldlings burst out in irritation, anger and bitter resentment when they feel that their rights are abused. The Christian must be different.

[28] As the apostle counsels, under such circumstances we need to keep our Lord or Master in mind, to remember his example. We need to be careful to accord Jesus Christ the greatest respect, assigning him a sacred place in our hearts. We are his disciples, and we want to speak to any interrogating authority as if we were standing in the very presence of our Lord. The reasons for our Christian position should be presented respectfully in a calm, even-tempered way.

GOOD EFFECT ON OPPOSERS

[29] Faithful endurance under suffering may also serve to silence opposers. The apostle Peter presents this as an incentive for preserving a clean conscience, saying: "Hold a good conscience, so that in the particular in which you are spoken against they may get ashamed who are speaking slightingly of your good conduct in connection with Christ." (1 Peter 3:16) Opposers observing the patient, uncomplaining manner in which God's servants act may become ashamed for having slandered them. This is especially the case when we treat opposers kindly.—Romans 12:19-21.

[30] The fact that such benefits can come from faithfully bearing up under affliction for the sake of righteousness adds force to Peter's next words: "For it is better to suffer because you are doing

29. What effect can a person's faithful endurance under suffering have on opposers?
30. (a) Why is there no benefit in suffering for doing evil? (b) In connection with suffering for righteousness' sake, why did Peter say, "if the will of God wishes it"?

good, if the will of God wishes it, than because you are doing evil." (1 Peter 3:17) What merit could there be in a person's suffering as a thief, an extortioner, a tax evader or as one who defies authority out of a false sense of piety or mistaken zeal? His being punished for this would only bring reproach on himself and his fellow believers. But a Christian's patiently bearing up under unjust mistreatment can impress others with the sustaining power that upholds true worshipers and can muzzle misrepresentations of God's truth and its upholders. Since the suffering that may befall a Christian comes on him by divine permission, Peter was not misrepresenting matters but said rightly, "if the will of God wishes it."

A REWARDING COURSE AS SHOWN IN JESUS' CASE

[31] That faithful endurance under suffering can lead to grand blessings for the Christian is well illustrated in the case of Jesus Christ. Sinless, he did nothing deserving of ill treatment. Yet his bearing up under affliction, finally to die a shameful death on a stake, worked out in marvelous benefits for us and resulted in his being richly rewarded. The apostle Peter wrote:

"Why, even Christ died once for all time concerning sins, a righteous person for unrighteous ones, that he might lead you to God, he being put to death in the flesh, but being made alive in the spirit. In this state also he went his way and preached to the spirits in prison, who had once been disobedient when the patience of God was waiting in Noah's days, while the ark was being constructed, in which a few people, that is, eight souls, were carried safely through the water." —1 Peter 3:18-20.

31. How did Jesus Christ's faithful endurance under suffering work out beneficially?

[32] It was because Jesus Christ maintained flawless integrity under suffering that he was able to lay down his life as a perfect human sacrifice. Thus his death paved the way for humans to be 'led to God,' being reconciled with the Most High and having set before them the prospect of everlasting life. In view of our having benefited so greatly from Christ's dying in our behalf, should we not be willing to follow his example and suffer for righteousness' sake?

[33] Moreover, just as in his case, we can rest assured that our faithful endurance will be blessed. The fact that Jesus Christ was "made alive in the spirit" or was resurrected to spirit life stands as an *unchangeable guarantee* that his disciples will be restored to life.—1 Corinthians 15:12-22.

[34] Because he came off the victor through faithful endurance, the Son of God, as a spirit person, was able to proclaim a message of judgment against the "spirits in prison." Since the disobedience of these spirits is linked with the time of Noah, they must be the angelic sons of God who left their original dwelling place in the heavens and took up living as husbands with women. (Genesis 6:1-4) They are spoken of as "spirits in prison" because their punishment included a form of restraint, being forever debarred from their original place among the faithful angels. The words of Jude confirm that only a message of condemnatory judgment could be directed to these fallen angels: "The angels that did not keep

32. How have we benefited from Christ's bearing up under suffering to the point of death?
33. Of what should the resurrection of Jesus Christ assure us when we are faced with the threat of death for being his disciples?
34. Because of his record of faithfulness, what was Jesus Christ able to do in connection with wicked spirits?

their original position but forsook their own proper dwelling place [God] has reserved with eternal bonds under dense darkness for the judgment of the great day." (Jude 6) It was Jesus' faithful endurance to the very death that entitled him to be restored to life and thus put him in a position to preach or proclaim such a condemnatory judgment to the fallen angels.

[35] This preaching of destruction for the wicked spirits should encourage us to endure faithfully when having to undergo affliction. Why? Because such wicked spirit forces are largely responsible for stirring up mankind alienated from God against the disciples of Jesus Christ. The Bible tells us: "The god of this system of things has blinded the minds of the unbelievers, that the illumination of the glorious good news about the Christ, who is the image of God, might not shine through." (2 Corinthians 4:4) "We [Christians] have a wrestling, not against blood and flesh, but against the governments, against the authorities, against the world rulers of this darkness, against the wicked spirit forces in the heavenly places." (Ephesians 6:12; see also Revelation 16:13, 14.) Hence, the fact that the resurrected Jesus Christ could preach a message of judgment against the wicked spirits provides the assurance that, eventually, their hateful influence will be totally abolished. (Compare Mark 1:23, 24.) What marvelous relief this will mean!

[36] Besides being raised from the dead as God's approved servant and thus enabled to direct a

---

35. Why can the fact about Jesus' preaching destruction to the "spirits in prison" encourage us to endure faithfully?
36. (a) How was Jesus Christ rewarded for his faithfulness? (b) In view of Jesus' position, how should we feel about suffering for the sake of his name?

message of judgment against the disobedient angels, Jesus Christ was highly exalted. The apostle Peter tells us: "He is at God's right hand, for he went his way to heaven; and angels and authorities and powers were made subject to him." (1 Peter 3:22) This statement agrees with Jesus' own words after his resurrection from the dead: "All authority has been given me in heaven and on the earth." (Matthew 28:18) Many persons have been willing to suffer and lay down life itself in the service of human rulers who had far, far less authority. They viewed it as a great honor to serve some king or queen in this way. How much more should we feel honored for being able to suffer for being loyal to our heavenly King, Jesus Christ!

IMITATE JESUS CHRIST

[37] Under affliction, then, look always to God's Son as your model. The apostle writes: "Since Christ suffered in the flesh, you too arm yourselves with the same mental disposition; because the person that has suffered in the flesh has desisted from sins, to the end that he may live the remainder of his time in the flesh, no more for the desires of men, but for God's will."—1 Peter 4:1, 2.

[38] What was Jesus' mental disposition? He humbly submitted to the physical and verbal abuse heaped on him, finally to die a painful death on a stake. By never retaliating in kind, the Son of God fulfilled the prophetic words: "As a sheep he was brought to the slaughter, and as a lamb

---

37. Whose example should we seek to imitate when experiencing affliction?
38. What was the mental disposition of Jesus Christ?

that is voiceless before its shearer, so he does not open his mouth."—Acts 8:32; Isaiah 53:7.

[39] We servants of the Most High would want to bear up similarly under suffering, not yielding to a spirit of rebellion or retaliation. For us to threaten our persecutors, to look for opportunities to do them harm, would show us up as still subject to the passions of the sinful flesh. Any suffering experienced at the hands of men should be solely because we do not follow the selfish course and ways of this world. (John 15:19, 25) Thus we can demonstrate that in attitude, word and action, we are living, "no more for the desires of men, but for God's will."

A REASON FOR HAPPINESS

[40] Back in the first century C.E., the idol-worshiping populace did not experience suffering for religious reasons. Any who became Christians, however, did become objects of hatred. To be subjected to persecution must have been a strange experience, puzzling. It was so different from the blessings that embracing the "good news" offered them. Those Christians very much needed the right perspective of affliction. The apostle Peter's following words were surely refreshing to them:

"Beloved ones, do not be puzzled at the burning among you, which is happening to you for a trial, as though a strange thing were befalling you. On the contrary, go on rejoicing forasmuch as you are sharers in the sufferings of the Christ, that you may rejoice and be overjoyed also during the revelation of his glory. If you are being reproached for

39. What proves that we have desisted from sins?
40. Why might it have seemed strange to many first-century believers to have to undergo suffering for the sake of Christ?

the name of Christ, you are happy, because the spirit of glory, even the spirit of God, is resting upon you."—1 Peter 4:12-14.

⁴¹ Instead of regarding with astonishment or surprise the affliction that may befall us, we may view it as being preparatory for our sharing in the blessings to be received at the revelation of our Master. Peter referred to the suffering as "burning," since metals are refined by fire. Similarly, God allows his servants to be refined or purified through the tribulations that they experience. Of course, Jehovah God did not make us sinful. But, since we are, he may permit us to experience certain suffering as one means of purifying us. The affliction that we may experience can aid us to become kinder, more humble, sympathetic and understanding in dealing with our fellow humans. Also, when we ourselves have endured severe trials, our words of comfort and encouragement to others carry far more weight. The ones whom we console know that we understand what they are going through.

⁴² Since the Son of God suffered, the afflictions we experience are a confirmation that we are really his disciples, enjoying a oneness with him. Jesus said to his apostles: "Bear in mind the word I said to you, A slave is not greater than his master. If they have persecuted me, they will persecute you also." (John 15:20) In being persecuted for the same reasons as was our Master and undergoing affliction for righteousness' sake as he did, we are 'sharing in the suffering of the Christ.' And just as his faithfulness led to his being rewarded by his heavenly Father, our con-

41, 42. (a) In harmony with 1 Peter 4:12-14, how might we regard suffering for the sake of righteousness? (b) What does such suffering confirm?

tinued faithfulness in bearing up under affliction assures us of being found approved at the revelation of the Son of God. Surely our joy will overflow at then being favored with endless life in a new order where all the causes of present sorrows are to be no more.

⁴³ As Peter also stated, the bearing of reproach for the name of Christ, that is, for being his disciples, should be a cause for happiness. It proves that those so reproached or defamed do have God's spirit or the honorable "spirit of glory" that emanates from God. Being holy, that spirit can rest only on persons who are clean or pure from God's standpoint.

⁴⁴ This is why it is so vital that we make sure that any suffering befalling us cannot be attributed to wrong action on our part. The apostle Peter urges: "However, let none of you suffer as a murderer or a thief or an evildoer or as a busybody in other people's matters."—1 Peter 4:15.

⁴⁵ A person who professes to be a Christian and who becomes guilty of a crime against his fellowman cannot expect exemption from some punishment. (Compare Acts 25:11.) That punishment will bring reproach on him, the congregation with which he is associated and the name of Christ. He gets, not joy, but shame.

⁴⁶ Meddling in the affairs of others can make one an object of hatred. How a person becomes a meddler is suggested by the Greek term for

---

43. Faithful endurance under suffering proves that we have what spirit upon us, and why?
44. What kind of suffering should we avoid?
45. What results when a professed Christian suffers for committing a crime?
46. (a) What is a busybody? (b) How might a Christian suffer as a busybody?

"busybody" that Peter used. It literally means an "overseer of what is another's." Perhaps because of having gained Scriptural knowledge, a Christian may now feel qualified to tell people of the world how to run their personal affairs. He may push his own opinions on standards of dress, disciplining children, handling marriage and sex problems, entertainment, diet and the like. When he injects himself, uninvited, into the personal problems of others, telling them what to do or not to do, he is trying to be an "overseer" of their affairs. This usually meets with resentment. The busybody may be told in no uncertain terms to mind his own business. He might even experience rough physical treatment from people who react angrily to his meddling in their private lives. The busybody who prys into matters that are not his concern brings trouble on his own head and misrepresents Christianity and its message to outsiders. Of course, even inside the congregation, there is no place for busybodies.—Compare 1 Timothy 5:13.

[47] In contrast to the shame of being publicly exposed as a lawbreaker or as a busybody, suffering as a Christian brings honor. Peter writes: "If he suffers as a Christian, let him not feel shame, but let him keep on glorifying God in this name." (1 Peter 4:16) When the affliction comes upon us because of our Christian way of life, our bearing up under it patiently and uncomplainingly brings glory to the Most High. It proves that what we have as Christians—a precious relationship with God and Christ, a clean conscience, spiritual well-being and a solid hope for the future—is a

---

47. How can a Christian's bearing up under suffering bring glory to God?

treasure of great worth. We show that we are willing to suffer and, if necessary, to die for it, and this glorifies the God we earnestly serve. To yield to pressure and renounce our faith would, instead, disgrace his name. To observers, it would call into serious question the inestimable value of being a disciple of Jesus Christ.—Compare Ephesians 3:13; 2 Corinthians 6:3-10.

A FORM OF DISCIPLINE OR TRAINING

[10] We have seen that unjust suffering by Christians could be prevented by Jehovah God in his all-powerfulness, but that he does permit it for good reasons. Meanwhile, the Most High never leaves his servants without help. In developing this point the apostle Peter writes:

> "For it is the appointed time for the judgment to start with the house of God. Now if it starts first with us, what will the end be of those who are not obedient to the good news of God? 'And if the righteous man is being saved with difficulty, where will the ungodly man and the sinner make a showing?' So, then, also let those who are suffering in harmony with the will of God keep on commending their souls to a faithful Creator while they are doing good."—1 Peter 4:17-19.

[49] As a "house of God," the Christian congregation had its beginning in 33 C.E. From that time onward its members have been under divine judgment. Their response to his will, and their attitude, words and actions toward the things that Jehovah God allows to befall them have much to do with what his final verdict will be. At times what Jehovah God sees fit to permit them to undergo

48. How does 1 Peter 4:17-19 show that we are not without help when undergoing suffering for the sake of righteousness?
49. (a) Since when has the "house of God" been under judgment? (b) What determines the final verdict that is rendered?

may be very severe. But the persecution brings a form of discipline that God can cause to work out for the benefit of his people.—Hebrews 12:4-11; see also Hebrews 4:15, 16, where it is shown that the suffering that Jesus Christ underwent equipped him to be a compassionate and sympathetic high priest.

⁵⁰ By mistreatment, men under the control of Satan may try to destroy our faith. But Jehovah can frustrate their wicked objective. Yes, while himself hating the bad, our heavenly Father can cause what is intended to harm us to work out to some good result. Take the case of Jacob's young son Joseph. His half brothers hated him and sold him into slavery. For years, Joseph suffered much, including unjust imprisonment. Yet, afterward, Jehovah God made use of this circumstance to preserve alive the family of Jacob. Regarding this, Joseph told his half brothers:

"Now do not feel hurt and do not be angry with yourselves because you sold me here; because *for the preservation of life God has sent me ahead of you.* For this is the second year of the famine in the midst of the earth, and there are yet five years in which there will be no plowing time or harvest. Consequently God sent me ahead of you in order to place a remnant for you men in the earth and to keep you alive by a great escape. So now it was not you who sent me here, but it was the true God, that he might appoint me a father to Pharaoh and a lord for all his house and as one dominating over all the land of Egypt."—Genesis 45:5-8.

⁵¹ Similarly, when the apostle Paul found himself in confinement at Rome, this unfavorable cir-

50, 51. How do the experiences of Joseph and Paul illustrate that Jehovah can turn into a blessing the very thing that men may use in an effort to harm us?

cumstance served to further the cause of true worship. In his letter to the Philippians, he wrote:

"Now I want to assure you, brothers, that what has happened to me has actually resulted in furthering the preaching of the good news. Thus it is generally known throughout the Imperial Guard and elsewhere that it is for the sake of Christ that I am in prison, and so most of the Christian brothers have been exceedingly encouraged by my example to declare God's message without any fear of the consequences."—Philippians 1:12-14, *An American Translation,* 1944 edition.

⁵² Since Jehovah God allows his loyal servants to undergo severe treatment to refine them and for them to demonstrate their devotion, how could we imagine that the "ungodly man and the sinner" inside the Christian congregation or "house of God" could even "make a showing" before Him along with "the righteous man" inside the same congregation? The psalmist states: "The wicked ones will not stand up in the judgment, nor sinners in the assembly of righteous ones." (Psalm 1:5) No, the wicked will not stand as approved but will be condemned. They may be found in the assembly of righteous ones, but they will never make a favorable "showing" before God. Because of what all believers must face in this world, their finally being saved for everlasting life takes real effort, love and faith in the way of righteousness. Hence, their salvation is "with difficulty." Consequently it behooves all members of the Christian congregation ("house of God") to avoid being "ungodly" and "sinners" in this "appointed time" of judgment.—1 Peter 4:17, 18; Proverbs 11:31.

---

52. Why can the "ungodly man and the sinner" not expect to make a showing?

⁵³ Trials that we simply could not endure in our own strength may befall us. However, no matter how pathetic our situation may become, Jehovah God can sustain us and totally undo all the hurt that we may experience. When we commit ourselves fully to him, he can strengthen us by means of his spirit to bear up under suffering. Being, as Peter states, a "faithful Creator," a God whom we can trust, he will not prove unfaithful to his promise to come to the aid of his servants. (1 Peter 4:19) This knowledge can help us to avoid reacting in a God-dishonoring way toward our persecutors. Instead of fighting against them, retaliating in kind, we will want to keep on doing good.—Luke 6:27, 28.

⁵⁴ If we humbly submit ourselves to what may befall us, maintaining a Christlike disposition, we can be confident that Jehovah will exalt us. No trial will continue indefinitely. It will have an end. As long as we conduct ourselves in harmony with the divine will while being subjected to ill treatment, we remain under Jehovah's hand. And that hand can lift us up, exalting us as his approved, tried servants. This is what the apostle Peter recommends: "Humble yourselves, therefore, under the mighty hand of God, that he may exalt you in due time; while you throw all your anxiety upon him, because he cares for you." —1 Peter 5:6, 7.

⁵⁵ How encouraging it is to know that Jehovah genuinely cares for us! His love warms our hearts;

53. (a) When undergoing suffering, what comfort can we draw from the fact that Jehovah is a "faithful Creator"? (b) How should we react toward our persecutors?
54. How do we humble ourselves under God's hand, and how does this benefit us?
55. Though we cannot run away from trials, of what can we relieve ourselves, and how?

his spirit strengthens and sustains us. Then, when a particular trial is over and we look back on Jehovah's loving care, we are drawn closer to him. The situation is comparable to that of an appreciative child that has experienced the love and care of concerned parents in a time of serious illness. His confidence and love are greatly strengthened. True, when circumstances are very trying, we cannot simply run away from them. But we can cast our anxiety or worry on Jehovah God. We do not need to fret as to how long we might be able to put up with a merciless beating by an enraged mob, sexual assaults by attackers, or other atrocities. With the help of our loving heavenly Father, we *can* endure and gain a moral victory over our persecutors by remaining faithful to our God. This assurance removes from us the anxiety that would rob us of the peace of mind and heart that is so essential in remaining firm in the face of trials.

[56] However, this does not mean that, by throwing our anxieties on Jehovah, we now can be complacent or indifferent. We do have an enemy. "Keep your senses, be watchful," Peter wrote. "Your adversary, the Devil, walks about like a roaring lion, seeking to devour someone."—1 Peter 5:8.

[57] In harmony with the apostle's counsel, we cannot afford to be careless in the face of afflictions. The adversary is just waiting for an opening to cause us to fall. If Satan can get us to doubt the faithfulness of our brothers or in some other way weaken us spiritually, he will do

56. Why does casting our anxieties upon Jehovah not mean that we can be unconcerned about our reaction to trials?
57. What is Satan interested in doing?

so. For us to withdraw from association with the Christian congregation or to stop making expression of our faith to others would mean being swallowed up by Satan, the "roaring lion" that is ever watchful for unwary prey.

[58] To maintain our alertness, it will help us to remember always that we are not alone in bearing up under suffering. Throughout the earth, our Christian brothers are putting up with various kinds of affliction. And, with the help of God's spirit, they are succeeding in faithfully enduring trials. This realization can aid us to avoid falling victim to Satan's snares, for it gives us confidence that we also can endure in the strength of Jehovah. So, then, "take your stand against him, solid in the faith, knowing that the same things in the way of sufferings are being accomplished in the entire association of your brothers in the world." —1 Peter 5:9.

[59] Since Jehovah God wants us to succeed and to gain salvation, we may confidently look to him for help. At the same time, we may accept whatever befalls us by God's permission as valuable discipline to make us complete, fully developed Christians, strong in faith. The apostle Peter beautifully expresses this, saying:

> "After you have suffered a little while, the God of all undeserved kindness, who called you to his everlasting glory in union with Christ, will himself finish your training, he will make you firm, he will make you strong. To him be the might forever. Amen."—1 Peter 5:10, 11.

[60] Just as Jesus Christ suffered for a little while on earth and was then highly exalted, so disciples

---

58. What knowledge about our brothers can aid us to remain faithful?
59, 60. How can we get the greatest benefit from our trials?

of God's Son look forward to a glorious reward. If
the suffering that may come upon us by divine
permission makes us stronger in our adherence to
Bible standards, and more humble, sympathetic
and compassionate disciples of God's Son, this
form of training or molding will have served its
purpose. For that to be the case, we need to trust
our heavenly Father fully, confident that whatever he allows to come will eventually secure our
eternal welfare and happiness if we humbly submit to it. (Romans 8:28) In the spirit of the apostle Peter, we can raise our voice, saying: 'Thanks
be to God for letting us be trained by trials and
helping us to be firm and strong as his approved
servants with everlasting life in view!'

9

Men Who Can Aid You to Succeed

A N ENCOURAGING word in time of distress, a helping hand when trouble threatens—what a blessing these can be! Because obstacles do arise to block our path as we move forward toward our goal of everlasting life, such aid is truly vital. It certainly is a blessing that in the Christian congregation there are faithful older brothers who can provide much-needed upbuilding and comfort.

[2] The Bible speaks of these "shepherds" as "gifts in men" whom Jesus Christ has provided for the building up of the congregation in love. (Ephesians 4:7-16) Therefore, if you should feel at any time that you are weakening in faith, are puzzled, perplexed or even disheartened because of problems or trials, you should call on devoted elders to help you stick to your decision to remain an approved disciple of God's Son.

[3] An examination of what the apostle Peter wrote to elders well illustrates how and why they can be a strengthening aid to you. We read:

"To the older men among you I give this exhortation, for I too am an older man with them and a witness of the sufferings of the Christ, a sharer even of the glory that is to be revealed: Shepherd

1, 2. (a) When faced with distress, what do we need from others? (b) In the Christian congregation, who especially can provide this?
3. What admonition is given to elders at 1 Peter 5:1-3?

the flock of God in your care, not under compulsion, but willingly; neither for love of dishonest gain, but eagerly; neither as lording it over those who are God's inheritance, but becoming examples to the flock."—1 Peter 5:1-3.

[4] We can rejoice that there are Christian men who want to conform to the apostle Peter's counsel. In providing spiritual help to members of the congregation, they render assistance in the same spirit as that shown by the apostle. Love for God and their brothers motivates them. Note that Peter did not exalt himself over the elders whom he was exhorting or encouraging. He spoke of himself as "an older man with them," that is, as a 'fellow elder.' The apostle thus referred to himself as a brother who had a sympathetic understanding of their position as elders in the congregation. Such a sympathetic attitude in dealing with fellow believers makes an elder a real blessing to his brothers.

[5] The words of Peter also show that he recognized the weighty responsibility that had been entrusted to him. He identified himself as a "witness of the sufferings of the Christ, a sharer even of the glory that is to be revealed." Peter knew firsthand about the way in which the Son of God was reviled, physically abused and finally nailed to a stake. He was a direct spectator and saw the resurrected Jesus Christ and his ascension to heaven. And in his second letter he says:

> "It was not by following artfully contrived false stories that we acquainted you with the power and presence of our Lord Jesus Christ, but it was by having become eyewitnesses of his magnificence.

4. How does Peter's language show that he did not exalt himself above the elders to whom he was writing?
5. How was Peter a "witness of the sufferings of the Christ"?

For he received from God the Father honor and glory, when words such as these were borne to him by the magnificent glory: 'This is my son, my beloved, whom I myself have approved.' Yes, these words we heard borne from heaven while we were with him in the holy mountain."—2 Peter 1:16-18; compare Matthew 16:28–17:9.

⁶ Surely, the elders to whom Peter was directing his encouragement had good reason to pay attention to the words of a fellow elder who could speak of himself as a 'witness of Christ's suffering and a sharer of the glory to be revealed.' Not only did the apostle appeal to them in a humble manner but his own example was worthy of imitation, for, as the Bible record shows, actively and at times with considerable danger to himself, he made known to others the things of which he was an eyewitness.—Acts 2:22-38; 4:8-12, 19, 20; 5:29-32.

⁷ For an elder today to be like Peter, he needs to recognize that the members of the congregation belong, not to him, but, to Jehovah God. The apostle Paul also called attention to this important fact. To the elders of the Ephesus congregation, he said: "Pay attention to yourselves and to all the flock, among which the holy spirit has appointed you overseers, to shepherd the congregation of God, which he purchased with the blood of his own Son."—Acts 20:28.

⁸ At great cost to himself, Jehovah God acquired the members of the Christian congregation as his property. No greater price could have been paid than that of the blood of his sinless Son. When elders have Jehovah's view of the value of the

6. Why did the elders whom Peter addressed have good reason to heed his words?
7, 8. (a) What should an elder recognize about the ownership of the flock? (b) How should this affect his treatment of the congregation?

congregation in their care, it aids them to be diligent in helping each individual to remain the honorable property of the Most High. They would have to answer to God for any mistreatment of the flock. That is why elders should endeavor to have a proper appreciation of the worth of each person in the congregation. This can serve as a strong restraint against taking a superior position toward the flock and treating it in a harsh, domineering way. (Contrast Acts 20:29.) Individually, members of the congregation are greatly built up by brothers who accord them the dignity and respect that is their due. It gives all a sense of security when elders prove themselves to be real "shepherds," looking out for the spiritual and physical well-being of the entire flock.

"NOT UNDER COMPULSION, BUT WILLINGLY"

⁹ In any given situation where help is needed, a person finds it much easier to approach someone who has not only the ability to render aid but also the *desire* to do so. Fittingly, Peter urged that the elders do their shepherding, "not under compulsion, but willingly." (1 Peter 5:2) To be a good "shepherd" in the congregation, a man needs to guard against performing his work merely out of a sense of duty. If caring for the congregation were to become joyless drudgery, an elder would simply be fulfilling an assignment "under compulsion." The flock would notice this and withdraw, not wanting to add to the elder's burdens with their problems. However, when an elder finds joy in handling his responsibilities because he

9, 10. (a) How might an elder do his shepherding "under compulsion"? (b) What would show that he is shepherding the congregation "willingly"?

really wants to do the work, the members of the congregation will be drawn to him. Such a willingness to serve stems from deep love for God and the congregation of his people. It is an evidence that the elder is accomplishing his ministry toward the flock with the right attitude.

[10] Of course, good judgment is needed on the part of an elder so that he does not burden himself down with more tasks than he can reasonably handle. With advancing years and declining health, he may not be able to accomplish as much as in former years, requiring that he ask other capable men to help him. Nevertheless, he may still find real joy in being a willing "shepherd" within the framework of his limitations.

'NOT FOR DISHONEST GAIN, BUT EAGERLY'

[11] Besides showing a willing spirit, an elder needs to have a pure, unselfish motivation if he is to be of real help to his brothers. The apostle Peter cautions against serving as a shepherd "for love of dishonest gain." To use one's shepherding assignment to gain material possessions, praise or power would be a dishonest use of it. True, the Bible counsels giving "double honor" to men who work hard at teaching. (1 Timothy 5:17, 18) But such "double honor" should always come *spontaneously* from congregation members, never being sought by an elder or viewed as something he rightly expects or exacts from them. Prominence may come to an elder, perhaps because his circumstances leave him free to share more extensively in Kingdom activity than others, or be-

---

11. Why is there a danger of shepherding the congregation "for love of dishonest gain"?

cause of certain outstanding abilities. There may easily arise a temptation to profit from his prominence, leading to his wanting, even hinting about, certain material things that others might be able to give him. This could perhaps lead to his associating mainly with more prosperous persons in the congregation, to the neglect of others. He may become desirous of praise but become cool, or even resentful, toward valid criticism or counsel.

¹² While this may happen to relatively few men in the Christian congregation today, elders should not minimize the danger. Even in very minor manifestations, the tendency to seek material benefits through spiritual relationships should be resisted. The Christian apostle Paul set an excellent example in this regard. To the elders of the Ephesus congregation, he could say:

"Bear in mind that for three years, night and day, I did not quit admonishing each one with tears. . . . I have coveted no man's silver or gold or apparel. You yourselves know that these hands have attended to the needs of me and of those with me. I have exhibited to you in all things that by thus laboring you must assist those who are weak, and must bear in mind the words of the Lord Jesus, when he himself said, 'There is more happiness in giving than there is in receiving.' "—Acts 20:31-35.

¹³ A congregation benefits immeasurably from men who labor "eagerly" as did Paul. He was glad to serve his brothers, never looking desiringly at anything that they possessed and from which he might benefit. His joy came from giving freely of himself in building up his brothers.

12, 13. How did the apostle Paul show that he served his brothers "eagerly"?

¹⁴ The unhypocritical way he and his companions served is made clear in his words to the Thessalonians:

"At no time have we turned up either with flattering speech, (just as you know) or with a false front for covetousness, God is witness! Neither have we been seeking glory from men, no, either from you or from others, though we could be an expensive burden as apostles of Christ. To the contrary, we became gentle in the midst of you, as when a nursing mother cherishes her own children. So, having a tender affection for you, we were well pleased to impart to you, not only the good news of God, but also our own souls, because you became beloved to us." (1 Thessalonians 2:5-8)

Yes, instead of seeking personal gain from members of the congregation, Paul acted as does a nursing mother who deeply loves her children and puts their interests ahead of her own.—Compare John 10:11-13.

¹⁵ In addition to being rightly motivated by concern for the flock, an elder needs to remember the importance of caring for the congregation in the right manner. The apostle Peter counseled that elders not 'lord it over those who are God's inheritance but that they become examples to the flock.' (1 Peter 5:3) In keeping with this admonition, elders would not lift themselves above their brothers. This would be contrary to the instructions that Jesus gave to his followers:

"Do not you be called Rabbi, for one is your teacher, whereas all you are brothers. Moreover, do not call anyone your father on earth, for one is your Father, the heavenly One. Neither be called

14. What do we learn from 1 Thessalonians 2:5-8 about what is included in shepherding the congregation "eagerly"?
15. In what manner should elders seek to shepherd the flock?

'leaders,' for your Leader is one, the Christ. But the greatest one among you must be your minister." (Matthew 23:8-11)

So, rather than issuing commands like a master, or trying to manage the lives of congregation members, an elder is a man who humbly slaves for his brothers. By his *example,* he encourages the flock to be Christlike.—Compare 1 Thessalonians 2:9-12.

¹⁶ When elders set a fine example personally in Christian living and activity, they can do much to assist their fellow believers finally to be found approved by Jehovah God. Moreover, Jesus Christ, the "chief shepherd" under whom they serve, will reward all faithful undershepherds at the time of his glorious manifestation as "King of kings and Lord of lords." (Revelation 19:16; 1 Timothy 6:15) As the apostle Peter wrote: "When the chief shepherd has been made manifest, you will receive the unfadable crown of glory." (1 Peter 5:4) Truly, men who serve their brothers for the right reason, with the proper motive and in the correct manner, are of real help to the congregation, contributing to their finding great joy in their Christian way of life. (2 Corinthians 1:24) Do not hesitate to enlist the aid of faithful elders whenever necessary.

---

16. Why can faithful elders be approached with confidence?

10

Safeguard Your Christian Hope

HOW grand to contemplate the prospect of life without pain, sorrow or death! And yet, in reality, it is even grander that our freedom from these things will come through the removal of imperfection and sin. What a blessing no longer to have to struggle against wrong leanings and tendencies that we know result only in injury to ourselves and others! It will indeed be a joy when every word we speak, every thought we think, every one of our actions will be for the good of all, genuinely reflecting what our heavenly Father is like, never stemming from selfish motives. Yes, for a certainty, righteousness will abound in the 'new heavens and the new earth' of God's making. Surely this is a hope worth safeguarding.—2 Peter 3:13.

² To see the fulfillment of our Christian hope, we need to keep it prominently before us and live in harmony with it. We can only do that if we resist all influences that could dim or destroy our hope. At times such damaging influence can come from unspiritual, self-seeking persons associated with the congregation of God's people. This should not

---

1. What will make the 'new heavens and the new earth' so desirable?
2. (a) To experience the fulfillment of our Christian hope, what must we do? (b) Why should we not be surprised that self-seeking men could be found among professing Christians?

surprise us, for the apostle Peter wrote: "There also came to be false prophets among the people [Israel], as there will also be false teachers among you [Christians]." (2 Peter 2:1a) Just as with natural Israel, Christians are subject to corruption from within the congregation.

"QUIETLY BRING IN DESTRUCTIVE SECTS"

3 Commenting on how the proponents of error operate, the apostle Peter continues: "These very ones will quietly bring in destructive sects." (2 Peter 2:1b) The apostle was not writing about persons who simply have difficulty in understanding certain matters, or persons whose views, honestly held, may not coincide in all respects with those of the majority. (Compare Romans 14:1-6.) He deals instead with those who *deliberately* work to divide and corrupt.

4 Such ones are seldom open, frank or straightforward. Generally they "bring in" their unscriptural views in a quiet, camouflaged way. In the original Greek used by the apostle Peter, the phrase "quietly bring in" is literally to "lead into by the side of, or along with." This is their method. Along with some sound Scriptural doctrine, they gradually and subtly introduce their divisive or corrupting views. By first conditioning the minds of their listeners with some obvious truths, or even by a long, involved line of reasoning, they can often get them to accept some principle that can lead only to error. They may *use* the Bible, but they do not really *teach* it, employing whatever they find convenient and slanting its teachings to fit what they, for personal advantage, are

---

3, 4. How does the apostle Peter describe the way in which false teachers propagate error?

trying to promote. Thus, what actually lacks any solid Scriptural foundation is made to appear to be true.

[5] This process is well illustrated in the way Satan deceived Eve by means of the serpent. Initially, a seemingly innocent question was raised: "Is it really so that God said you must not eat from every tree of the garden?" (Genesis 3:1) That question perverted the truth. It intimated that the Most High was unduly restrictive, withholding from the first humans something to which they were entitled. The serpent's words must have caused Eve to wonder just why she could not eat from the "tree of the knowledge of good and bad." In this way Satan conditioned her mind to want an answer. Then came the serpent's pointed reply: "You positively will not die. For God knows that in the very day of your eating from it your eyes are bound to be opened and you are bound to be like God, knowing good and bad."—Genesis 3:4, 5.

[6] Since Eve's mind had been subtly prepared for it, the lying answer did not come as a shock. The fact that "the serpent proved to be the most cautious" of all the animals seemed to suggest that such a creature could hardly be the source of wrong information. (Genesis 3:1) Furthermore, the tree was attractive and its fruit gave indication of being good for food. Eve was totally deceived. After partaking of the forbidden fruit, she persuaded Adam to join her in rebellion against God. (Genesis 3:6) In this way the lying words of the

---

5. How does Satan's manner in deceiving Eve illustrate the methods of a teacher of falsehood?
6. (a) What factors made Eve susceptible to accepting error? (b) How was a heretical body formed as a result of Satan's lie?

serpent succeeded in alienating the first humans from their heavenly Father. In actuality, a heretical body consisting of two persons was formed.

⁷ By similar means, men may foment a divisive spirit in a congregation, a "party" spirit of rivalry. Since any such faction has its roots in error and deliberately seeks to create disunity, its stand and teachings misrepresent the Son of God, who bought the Christian congregation with his blood. Therefore, the apostle Peter speaks of such pseudo teachers as 'disowning even the owner that bought them, bringing speedy destruction upon themselves.' Yes, once people stop holding fast to Christ as head, they disown him and plunge into a course that is morally and spiritually disastrous. There can be only one outcome—destruction. When the time for executing condemnatory judgment comes, there will be no delay. Justice will be executed swiftly. By willingly embracing error, the individuals involved 'bring speedy destruction upon themselves.'—2 Peter 2:1.

⁸ Sadly, these persons, because they claim to be Christians while conducting themselves in an unbridled way, put a blot on the fine record of God's faithful servants. Many who observe the debased conduct of certain individuals professing to be Christians begin to speak blasphemously or abusively of all who identify themselves as being such. This is the point that Peter made when he wrote: "Furthermore, many will follow their acts of loose conduct, and on account of these the way of the truth will be spoken of abusively."—2 Peter 2:2.

---

7. (a) Why do those who cause divisions in the congregation disown Christ? (b) Why can it be said that they 'bring speedy destruction upon themselves'?
8. What effect can the "loose conduct" of professed Christians have on persons outside the congregation?

BEWARE OF BEING 'EXPLOITED
WITH COUNTERFEIT WORDS'

[9] What motivates such corrupt men to build up a following for themselves? The apostle Peter answers: "With covetousness they will exploit you with counterfeit words." (2 Peter 2:3a) These individuals seek to gain material advantages for themselves or want the power, authority and honor that come with being looked up to as teachers. By means of "counterfeit words," that is, deceitful statements, including plausible arguments, they endeavor to take advantage of others, exploiting them. Since both the motivations and the teachings are wrong, the result to the individuals involved is ruin. The apostle Peter continues:

"As for them, the judgment from of old is not moving slowly, and the destruction of them is not slumbering. Certainly if God did not hold back from punishing the angels that sinned, but, by throwing them into Tartarus, delivered them to pits of dense darkness to be reserved for judgment; and he did not hold back from punishing an ancient world, but kept Noah, a preacher of righteousness, safe with seven others when he brought a deluge upon a world of ungodly people; and by reducing the cities Sodom and Gomorrah to ashes he condemned them, setting a pattern for ungodly persons of things to come; and he delivered righteous Lot, who was greatly distressed by the indulgence of the law-defying people in loose conduct—for that righteous man by what he saw and heard while dwelling among them from day to day was tormenting his righteous soul by reason of their lawless deeds —Jehovah knows how to deliver people of godly devotion out of trial, but to reserve unrighteous people for the day of judgment to be cut off, especially, however, those who go on after flesh with the desire to defile it and who look down on lordship."—2 Peter 2:3-10.

9. (a) What motivates corrupt men to try to build up a following? (b) What will happen to such men and those who are deceived by them?

¹⁰ The executional judgment that God has decreed "from of old" against all who come to belong to the 'serpent's seed' will without fail be carried out. (Genesis 3:15; John 8:44; Jude 14, 15) Though originally stated about 6,000 years ago and repeated since then, this judgment is "not moving slowly" as if it will never arrive. The destruction is sure to come, for it is not dormant. It is still very much alive in God's purpose.

¹¹ As Peter noted, even angels who had enjoyed being in the very presence of God but who later became unfaithful were not spared being 'thrown into Tartarus,' that is, debased to the lowest degree. Cut off from all divine enlightenment, debarred from their original position in the heavens and limited in their activities, the disobedient angels find themselves in a condition comparable to "pits of dense darkness," awaiting executional judgment at the hands of Jesus Christ. (Compare Revelation 20:1-3, 7-10.) Similarly, Jehovah God did not hold back from destroying an entire world of corrupt people in a global flood nor from acting against the sexually depraved inhabitants of Sodom and Gomorrah in the days of Lot. Only righteous persons like Noah and his family and like Lot can hope to escape divine judgment and be delivered from the trial resulting from living among lawless persons. However, claims of being Christian will not save anyone who seeks to defile the flesh of others by committing immorality.

---

10. (a) When was the first expression of God's judgment against the 'serpent's seed' made? (b) Why is its execution "not moving slowly"?

11. (a) What happened to the disobedient angels, and what still awaits them? (b) What is proved by the punishment of the angels, the destruction of the ungodly in the Flood, and the annihilation of the inhabitants of Sodom and Gomorrah?

BE ON GUARD
AGAINST THOSE WHO DISRESPECT AUTHORITY

[12] Often the bad motivations of corrupt persons can be discerned by their attitude toward authority. They "look down on lordship," despising authority of any kind. The apostle Peter continues his description: "Daring, self-willed, they do not tremble at glorious ones but speak abusively, whereas angels, although they are greater in strength and power, do not bring against them an accusation in abusive terms, not doing so out of respect for Jehovah."—2 Peter 2:10b, 11.

[13] Therefore, we would want to beware of bold, presumptuous men who have no regard for "glorious ones." In the Christian congregation, faithful men entrusted with responsibility do not view themselves as being of superior rank or as being exalted above fellow believers but humbly regard themselves as servants. (Matthew 23:8; 1 Thessalonians 2:5-12) However, their assignment of service is a 'glorious one,' as they are appointed by holy spirit as overseers or "shepherds" of the flock. (Acts 20:28; compare Romans 11:13.) They also represent the glorious Lord Jesus Christ and the Great Shepherd Jehovah God. (1 Peter 2:25; 5:4) That is why the Scriptures encourage members of the congregation to be submissive to those who are taking the lead. (Hebrews 13:17) While such men, like Peter himself, may make mistakes, this would not excuse anyone who speaks in an abusive way against them. (Compare Galatians 2:11-14; 3 John 9, 10.) Hardworking "shepherds" deserve the respect of the congregation. But men who influence others for bad do not shrink back

12, 13. As shown at 2 Peter 2:10b, 11, what is the attitude of corrupt persons toward authority?

from reviling Christian elders. If a person uses abusive, reviling speech against his brother, Jehovah God and his Son count it as if done to themselves.

¹⁴ How different self-seeking teachers of falsehood are from the faithful angels! The angels have a zeal for righteousness. But they do not use harsh, abusive language even when dealing with opposers. For example, "when Michael the archangel had a difference with the Devil and was disputing about Moses' body, he did not dare to bring a judgment against him in abusive terms, but said: 'May Jehovah rebuke you.'" (Jude 9) From this we can conclude that the other faithful angels would never resort to heaping reproaches on anyone but would calmly, yet forcefully, set forth the facts. They have a proper regard for their Maker, realizing that abusive speech is never in harmony with his holiness or purity.

¹⁵ We must be on guard against persons who viciously downgrade others and then proceed to advance themselves. The fact that such individuals will not escape adverse judgment for their actions should remain prominently before us. This can aid us to be cautious in lending an ear to those who seem to be interested in others but are, in reality, only seeking their personal advantage. The apostle Peter commented on the outcome for self-seeking men, saying:

> "These men, like unreasoning animals born naturally to be caught and destroyed, will, in the things of which they are ignorant and speak abusively,

---

14. How do the faithful angels show an entirely different attitude from that of false teachers?
15. In harmony with Peter's counsel, against what kind of persons must we be on guard?

even suffer destruction in their own course of destruction, wronging themselves as a reward for wrongdoing."—2 Peter 2:12, 13a.

[16] Men who are ruled by vicious passions act like "unreasoning animals." Concerning animals Jehovah said: "Every moving animal that is alive may serve as food for you." (Genesis 9:3) In being like such "unreasoning animals," the abusively speaking men are not bridled by the dictates of a good conscience and so show no appreciation for God's ways, dealings and activities. Unable to make a proper estimation of valuable spiritual things, they may speak of them as being worthless. Their wrong opinions will be their undoing. They hold to these false views to their own injury and are bound to experience the bad results of their unrighteous course. Surely, we want to hold fast to our hope and avoid sharing in their ruin.

BEWARE OF THOSE WHO SEEK
SELFISH PLEASURE AND PERSONAL GAIN

[17] Among other bad traits, unspiritual persons have a burning desire for ease and pleasure. The apostle Peter wrote:

"They consider luxurious living in the daytime a pleasure. They are spots and blemishes, indulging with unrestrained delight in their deceptive teachings while feasting together with you. They have eyes full of adultery and unable to desist from sin, and they entice unsteady souls. They have a heart trained in covetousness. They are accursed children. Abandoning the straight path, they have been misled."—2 Peter 2:13b-15a.

16. How are corrupt men like "unreasoning animals"?
17. According to 2 Peter 2:13b-15a, what are some other identifying traits of corrupt men?

¹⁸ During the daylight hours, when they could be accomplishing much for the upbuilding of others, unspiritual persons may instead engage in revelries, giving themselves over to excesses in food and drink. They are much like certain Israelites who lived solely for pleasure. Wine flowed with excessive freedom at their feasts. As the day progressed into the night, the revelers would become louder and more boisterous, accompanying their noisy feasting with passion-arousing music. The prophet Isaiah writes of such ones:

> "Woe to those who are getting up early in the morning that they may seek just intoxicating liquor, who are lingering till late in the evening darkness so that wine itself inflames them! And there must prove to be harp and stringed instrument, tambourine and flute, and wine at their feasts; but the activity of Jehovah they do not look at, and the work of his hands they have not seen." (Isaiah 5:11, 12)

The pleasure seekers thus acted as if no testimony existed as to the grand works of the Creator. They exercised no restraint, ignoring all accountability to Jehovah God, and, therefore, could not hope to escape his judgment.

¹⁹ It should not surprise us if similar things should take place among some persons who claim to be God's servants today. Wedding receptions and anniversaries may be converted into occasions for wild, sensuous dancing to the blare of passion-arousing music. At such celebrations, alcoholic beverages may flow too freely. The loud, unruly partying may not end until the wee hours of the morning or until daybreak. In some lands, the

---

18. How are unspiritual persons like the unfaithful Israelites described in Isaiah 5:11, 12?
19. What shows that some persons associated with the congregation are lovers of pleasures?

naming of a newborn child, the inauguration of a new house, funerals and the dedication of buildings used for worship may be converted into occasions for holding gatherings that become very inconsiderate, disturbing even worldly neighbors and causing them to appeal for relief from the excessive noise. Even in lands where people are generally known for their reserve, heavy drinking may develop among close friends in a way that causes the truth of the "good news" to be spoken of with contempt. Surely, true Christians must guard against such excesses.—1 Peter 4:3.

²⁰ As the apostle Peter said, those acting in this way are like spots and blemishes on the Christian congregation. They mar the clean appearance of God's true servants. They are like spots on a clean garment or like any unsightly blemish on an otherwise attractive face. Because the intent of certain persons is to 'go all out' to satisfy their desire for pleasure, they turn even normally fine occasions into rowdy ones. They try to influence or to teach others to join them in wild dancing and heavy drinking by claiming it is just 'normal relaxation.' The "eyes full of adultery" Peter refers to may be in evidence. At social affairs, male eyes may begin to look with immoral interest at attractive women present. The impure desires may become so powerful that the eyes even of married men simply cannot fail to be guilty of sinning. (Compare Matthew 5:28; Mark 9:47.) Women who are not firmly established in Christian principles, as "unsteady souls," may easily become the victims of corrupt men.—Compare 2 Timothy 3:6, 7.

---

20. (a) What effect do those who are given to excesses have on the congregation? (b) How are even noble occasions turned into carouses?

²¹ These men are a real danger, for they show skill in enticing the weak. The apostle Peter describes them as 'having a heart *trained* in covetousness.' Their whole objective or aim in life seems to be the satisfying of covetous desires, and they become experts in achieving their ends. The disciple Jude also spoke of such ones who 'slip in' and turn God's undeserved kindness "into an excuse for loose conduct," thereby proving false to our only Owner, Jesus Christ. He shows that they often 'admire personalities for the sake of their own benefit,' and that those causing divisions are "animalistic men, not having spirituality." (Jude 4, 16, 19) If any succeed, whether by flattery or by some display of apparent zeal, in gaining influence or prominence within a congregation, they pose a grave danger. Rightly such ones come under God's curse and merit destruction, even as the apostle Peter declares. What is true of men who follow this divisive, corrupting course would be equally true of women who do so.—Compare Revelation 2:20-23.

²² The apostle Peter also compared corrupt men to Balaam, saying:

> "They have followed the path of Balaam, the son of Beor, who loved the reward of wrongdoing, but got a reproof for his own violation of what was right. A voiceless beast of burden, making utterance with the voice of a man, hindered the prophet's mad course." (2 Peter 2:15b, 16)

This diviner knew full well that it was contrary to the will of the Supreme Sovereign to curse the Israelites. While outwardly maintaining that he

---

21. Why are persons who would involve others in a life of excesses a real danger to the Christian congregation?
22, 23. How are those who corrupt others like Balaam?

would not go beyond what Jehovah would impel him to speak, Balaam was inwardly nurturing the desire to curse Israel. He wanted the reward that Moabite King Balak offered. But the Almighty God reproved Balaam by means of Balaam's own she-ass. By a miracle, the Most High caused an unreasoning beast of burden to utter intelligible speech. (Numbers 22:1-35) This was no difficult thing for the One who could make even the stones cry out. (Luke 19:40) In view of Balaam's extreme greed for gain, Jehovah God rightly employed this most unusual means of reproof. In trying to resist God's will respecting Israel, Balaam acted like a man lacking his senses. For a time, the reproof of his domestic animal hindered him from pursuing his course, as it showed that he simply could not succeed in cursing Israel. —Numbers 23:1–24:9.

[23] Nevertheless, Balaam was still bent on getting the reward. Finally, he came up with a plan whereby the Israelites would bring God's curse upon themselves. He instructed Balak as to how he could use Moabite and Midianite women to get the men of Israel to engage in idolatry and fornication. (Numbers 31:16; Revelation 2:14) The scheme had a measure of success and was responsible for the death of 24,000 Israelites.—Numbers 25:1-9.

[24] How forcefully the case of Balaam illustrates the course of men who forsake what is right for personal gain! Not even a miracle would stop them from trying to satisfy their greediness. Therefore, we should avoid close association with anyone whose attitude, speech and conduct seriously dis-

---

24. What does the example of Balaam help us to see about persons who are self-seeking?

turb our conscience. Self-seeking men simply have no qualms about injuring others to attain their own goals.

[25] Continuing his description of such wicked men, Peter states: "These are fountains without water, and mists driven by a violent storm, and for them the blackness of darkness has been reserved." (2 Peter 2:17) Nothing beneficial can be gained through close fellowship with defiled persons. They are like wells or fountains that a weary traveler might approach in the hope of getting refreshing water, only to be disappointed to find that the source of water is dried up. They are also like wispy, mistlike clouds that one might look to in hope of needed rain for growing crops but which are quickly blown away by strong winds. Teachers of falsehood are not the source of any light or enlightenment. They themselves are headed for the "blackness of darkness," a total darkness representative of the condemnatory judgment that awaits them.

BE CAREFUL OF "SWELLING EXPRESSIONS"

[26] It is because of their deceptive outward appearance that we must be on guard against dangerous elements inside the congregation. Especially those who are not well established in Christian truth and living must be careful. The methods employed by self-seeking men may be very impressive. But woe to those who are deceived by their grandiose persuasions! The apostle Peter says:

"They utter swelling expressions of no profit, and by the desires of the flesh and by loose habits

---

25. What is emphasized by the words of 2 Peter 2:17?
26. How does the apostle Peter describe the way in which corrupt men attain their ends?

they entice those who are just escaping from people who conduct themselves in error. While they are promising them freedom, they themselves are existing as slaves of corruption. For whoever is overcome by another is enslaved by this one."—2 Peter 2:18, 19.

²⁷ Those who persuade others to adopt error or to follow a course contrary to the dictates of a clean conscience often speak with great conviction. They think very highly of themselves and their words, attaching great weight to their utterances. (Compare 2 Corinthians 10:10, 12; 11:3-6, 12, 13.) Instead of presenting sound Scriptural reasons in a spirit of humility, they may ridicule and speak out in a forceful, pompous manner, concealing the weakness of their argument with bluster. (Contrast 2 Corinthians 4:2.) When examined in the light of the Holy Scriptures, their impressive words are shown to be empty or of no benefit to anyone.

²⁸ Sadly, those who are not firmly grounded in the Word of God may not recognize the danger. Their 'perceptive powers are not trained to distinguish right from wrong.' (Hebrews 5:14) Since it may have been quite recently that these unsteady ones separated themselves from God-dishonoring practices carried on in the world, such practices may still have some appeal to them.

²⁹ Clearly, there is need for balance in our approach to matters of entertainment and recreation. The Scriptures do not call upon God's servants to live a life of asceticism, nor do they represent self-

27. What is characteristic of the speech and attitude of persons who exert a corrupting influence?
28. Who are most likely to be influenced by corrupt elements inside the congregation?
29. What is the Scriptural view of entertainment or recreation, and just when do we need to be on guard?

denial as having virtue *in itself* but only when it is engaged in with some good objective in view. (Compare Ecclesiastes 2:24; 3:1, 4, 13; 8:15; 1 Corinthians 13:3; Colossians 2:20-23.) But this does not give any excuse for going to extremes, letting the fallen flesh take control and using Christian freedom as a cloak for badness. (Galatians 5:13, 14; 1 Peter 2:16) Such a course can never be harmonized with the love of God and the love of one's neighbor as oneself, the "kingly law" that we are under. (James 2:8, 12) Those who argue otherwise, and who ridicule those who do not agree with them in their excesses, show they are still slaves to their own selfish leanings.

[30] So there is need to keep our senses and avoid both extremes. There is an undeniable danger of being led into a course of heedless pursuit of pleasure. One can gradually be pulled into a whirlpool of parties that, over a period of time, deteriorate in quality, slipping more and more into extremes in dancing or drinking, or of viewing entertainment that glorifies sexual immorality and sadism. It is unreasoning to claim that these unwholesome influences pose no danger. They can hardly help but have a weakening effect on the Christian conscience, breaking down one's moral fiber. Persons pretending otherwise often wind up as victims to drunkenness and sexual misconduct. —Proverbs 13:20.

[31] Truly, the apostle Peter accurately depicted what will continue to happen among God's servants until "the day of judgment [for unrighteous

30. What can eventually happen because of corrupt influence inside the congregation?
31, 32. What will some members of the congregation continue to do until "the day of judgment" and with what consequences?

people] to be cut off." (2 Peter 2:9) There will always be persons who try to extend the limits of Christian freedom far beyond what is reasonable so that they can satisfy their desires for sensual pleasure. They do not want to follow the Biblical injunction: "Deaden, therefore, your body members that are upon the earth as respects fornication, uncleanness, sexual appetite, hurtful desire, and covetousness." (Colossians 3:5) Instead, they choose the very entertainment that incites these wrong desires. When involving others, they may argue: 'If our conscience allows it, there is nothing wrong with it.' But they fail to recognize that a *defiled* conscience is not a safe guide. These persons are yielding to their wrong desires and are, therefore, in slavery to these. Their promises of "freedom" to others are misleading.

[32] The result to those who are again plunged into a life of wrongdoing is indeed calamitous. The apostle Peter wrote:

> "Certainly if, after having escaped from the defilements of the world by an accurate knowledge of the Lord and Savior Jesus Christ, they get involved again with these very things and are overcome, the final conditions have become worse for them than the first. For it would have been better for them not to have accurately known the path of righteousness than after knowing it accurately to turn away from the holy commandment delivered to them. The saying of the true proverb has happened to them: 'The dog has returned to its own vomit, and the sow that was bathed to rolling in the mire.' "—2 Peter 2:20-22.

[33] Why could the apostle Peter say this? Once a person gains accurate knowledge of the Lord

---

33. (a) What changes may a person make upon coming to a knowledge of the truth? (b) Why is a return to the ways of the world a very serious matter?

Jesus Christ, he begins to see the need for making changes. He may give up heavy drinking, a life of immorality, gambling and other vices. By cleaning himself up to conform to what is expected of a disciple of Jesus Christ, the individual flees or escapes from the "defilements of the world," from practices that he has come to know as being divinely disapproved. However, on again becoming entangled in God-dishonoring practices, he deliberately throws aside what he knows to be right. His knowledge of Jesus Christ and his Bible-trained conscience initially served as a restraint against wrong conduct. When breaking free from that wholesome restraint, he may well become even worse than before he took up the way of Christian discipleship. He may go beyond what men do who have no knowledge of the path of righteousness. This is because his conscience has become contaminated, or even scarred—like dead tissue. (Compare 1 Timothy 4:2.) If he had never known the right path, his bad conduct would not have disgraced so terribly the name of Christ, his sin would not have had the same gravity, and the divine judgment against him would not have needed to be as severe.—Compare Luke 12:45-48; 1 Timothy 1:13, 15, 16.

[34] In view of the proverb that Peter quotes, those who take up a life of sin evidently fail to use their opportunities to advance in Christian living. (2 Peter 1:2-11) Some may outwardly abandon bad practices but never come to hate these. They may not really leave behind the "vomit," the filth, of this world. To them, there still is something at-

34, 35. (a) What can we draw from the proverb about the unclean dog and the pig? (b) What should this proverb impress on us?

tractive about it, and so they can be induced to turn back to it. They may have an inward desire to roll around in the world's mire of moral degradation. In the case of others, they may fail to increase in appreciation for the value of Christian discipleship, and eventually what the world has to offer takes on greater appeal. How tragic is the fall of those who are thus lured back into the state that had at one time been sickening to them!

[35] The inspired proverb stands as a warning lesson to all who claim to be Christian. If we are not cultivating moral and spiritual cleanness in our hearts and lack a real loathing for the filth of this world, we are in grave danger of spiritual ruin. Christians simply cannot afford to let down their guard in resisting the enticements of a corrupt world. We must deaden our wrong desires, not allowing them to gain the mastery over us, nor should we stimulate them by looking with longing to what the world has to offer.—1 Corinthians 10:12; Colossians 3:5.

REMAIN AWAKE!

[36] Besides remaining morally and spiritually clean, we also need to be active in the service of our Master, helping others spiritually as well as materially. Our whole course of life should reflect spiritual wakefulness and activity. Emphasizing the importance of this, the apostle Peter stated:

"Beloved ones, this is now the second letter I am writing you, in which, as in my first one, I am arousing your clear thinking faculties by way of a reminder, that you should remember the sayings previously spoken by the holy prophets and the

---

36. Besides remaining morally and spiritually clean, what do we need to do to please our Master?

commandment of the Lord and Savior through your apostles. For you know this first, that in the last days there will come ridiculers with their ridicule, proceeding according to their own desires and saying: 'Where is this promised presence of his? Why, from the day our forefathers fell asleep in death, all things are continuing exactly as from creation's beginning.' "—2 Peter 3:1-4.

37 Certainly we today benefit from having our 'clear thinking faculties aroused' so that we can make a proper evaluation of what is essential for gaining divine approval. (Compare 2 Peter 1:12-15.) The "holy prophets" as far back as Enoch warned of a day of reckoning. At Jude 14, 15, we read: "Yes, the seventh one in line from Adam, Enoch, prophesied also regarding them, when he said: 'Look! Jehovah came with his holy myriads, to execute judgment against all, and to convict all the ungodly concerning all their ungodly deeds that they did in an ungodly way, and concerning all the shocking things that ungodly sinners spoke against him.' " Centuries later, Hebrew prophets such as Isaiah, Daniel, Joel, Habakkuk, Zephaniah, Haggai, Zechariah and Malachi were moved to utter similar prophecies.—Isaiah 66:15, 16; Daniel 7:9-22; Joel 3:9-17; Habakkuk 3:16-18; Zephaniah 1:14-18; Haggai 2:21, 22; Zechariah 14:6-9; Malachi 4:1-6.

38 The divine judgment foretold by all these prophets and others is bound to be fulfilled. This requires that we at all times strive to be in a state of preparedness and not jeopardize our clean standing before the Most High.

---

37. (a) Why should we have our 'clear thinking faculties aroused'? (b) To what momentous event did the prophets point?
38. Why should we strive to be in a state of preparedness?

[39] The message of the prophets to us is the same as that conveyed by the commandment of our Lord Jesus Christ, as repeated by the apostles, including Paul. We disciples of the Son of God should be active in his service, remain morally and spiritually clean, and be always ready to receive our Master when he comes to execute judgment against the ungodly. The Son of God stated:

"Pay attention to yourselves that your hearts never become weighed down with overeating and heavy drinking and anxieties of life, and suddenly that day be instantly upon you as a snare. For it will come in upon all those dwelling upon the face of all the earth. Keep awake, then, all the time making supplication that you may succeed in escaping all these things that are destined to occur, and in standing before the Son of man."—Luke 21:34-36.

[40] Yes, we must guard against being plunged into spiritual sleep. This calls for avoiding unrestrained indulgence in food, drink and pleasures. Such excesses dull mental and spiritual perception and overload the heart with feelings of guilt. They crowd out good heart motivations. Similarly, undue concern about making a living can rob the heart of the calming assurance that Jehovah God will provide everything that we truly need. (Matthew 6:25-34) Whenever the main motivation of the heart ceases to be the desire to be found approved by the Lord Jesus Christ at his time for judgment, a person comes into a condition of grave spiritual danger. He may be caught in a disapproved state by the Master, Jesus Christ.

39. What is the message conveyed by the commandment of Jesus Christ?
40. To avoid being plunged into spiritual sleep, what must we do?

⁴¹ Like Peter, the other faithful apostles taught their fellow believers to keep ever before them the certainty of Christ's coming to execute judgment and to reward his loyal disciples. A prime objective of such teaching was to aid Christians to be found approved on the Son's arrival "with power and great glory." (Matthew 24:30) As Jesus had done, the apostles continued to emphasize the importance of proving faithful to the end. That end could come either at their death or at "the presence of the day of Jehovah." (2 Peter 3:12) Since even the resurrection of Christ's joint heirs is linked in the Scriptures with his return, the hopes of all true disciples are bound up with the arrival of the Son of God in the capacity of a glorious heavenly King. (Matthew 10:28; 24:13, 36-44; 1 Thessalonians 1:9, 10; 4:14-17) Thus, during the entire history of the Christian congregation, unshakable faith in the Master's coming "with power and great glory" has been an aid in a person's proving loyal to him.

DO NOT BE DECEIVED BY RIDICULERS

⁴² Partly because of eagerness to be alive when Jesus Christ reveals himself in glory, there have been believers throughout the centuries who began looking to a particular period or a year for the windup of the ungodly system of things. This has happened right down to these "last days." Since certain expectations were not realized, many stumbled and returned to the ways of the world. In fulfillment of Peter's words, even today we hear the voice of ridiculers. (2 Peter 3:3, 4) In

41. Why has faith in the certainty of Christ's coming in glory always been an aid in a person's remaining loyal to him?
42. (a) Why do we hear the voice of ridiculers today? (b) What is their argument?

effect, they say: 'What reason is there to believe that the Son of God is going to execute the ungodly and to reward his disciples? Why, nothing has changed since the time of creation. The original processes of life are continuing and give no indication of coming to a disastrous end in the near future. Men are marrying, and women are being given in marriage, babies are being born, and men continue to grow old and die.' Thus they imply that the Lord Jesus Christ never will come to execute judgment or that this event is so far off in the future that it is of no immediate concern.

[43] Such ridiculers have totally lost sight of the fact that either death or "the day of Jehovah" will inescapably overtake them. In either event, they will have no further opportunity to lay up treasure in heaven in the form of fine works. (Luke 12:15-21, 31, 33-40) Hence, for disciples of Jesus Christ there has never been a period of history when they could afford to be neglectful of their responsibilities. Certainly, the risk in doing so is even greater in our time.

[44] Today, then, just what responsibilities should we be discharging? For one thing, we are under command to "make disciples of people of all the nations, baptizing them in the name of the Father and of the Son and of the holy spirit, teaching them to observe all the things I have commanded." (Matthew 28:19, 20) Yes, at the conclusion of the system of things, we are privileged to share in the worldwide preaching of the "good news of the kingdom." (Matthew 24:14) Of particularly vital importance at this time is our obligation to

---

43. What shows that there has always been a need for Christ's disciples to be diligent in discharging their responsibilities?
44. What basic responsibilities should we be discharging?

show love to all our brothers, responding to their needs for assistance, sympathy and encouragement. (Compare Matthew 25:35-40; Hebrews 13: 1-3; 1 John 3:16-18.) Moreover, we need to exert ourselves constantly to remain clean from the degrading works of the flesh.—Matthew 7:21-23; Galatians 5:19-21.

JEHOVAH HAS PROVED
THE RIDICULERS TO BE WRONG

45 As we continue leading a life that harmonizes with our being disciples of Jesus Christ, we will want to keep ever before us that Jehovah God long ago provided the evidence that undeniably proves the ridiculers to be wrong. Calling attention to this fact, the apostle Peter wrote:

"According to their wish, this fact escapes their notice, that there were heavens from of old and an earth standing compactly out of water and in the midst of water by the word of God; and by those means the world of that time suffered destruction when it was deluged with water."—2 Peter 3:5, 6.

46 The fact that Jehovah God once before destroyed a world of ungodly people shows that the ridiculers are wrong in concluding that there will be no drastic change in human affairs but that all things will continue "exactly as from creation's beginning." We have God's own word of promise that, by means of his Son, he will take action against the ungodly. That word is so powerful that there is no possibility of its failing to be fulfilled.

47 The manner in which the Bible speaks of Jehovah's creative works reveals the power of

45, 46. What evidence has Jehovah provided to show that the ridiculers are wrong?
47. How does the creation account reveal the power of God's "word"?

his "word." From Genesis chapter 1, we learn that, when the Most High says the word or gives the command, his purpose is as good as accomplished. (Compare Psalm 148:1-6.) With reference to the second day, we are told: "God went on to say: 'Let an expanse come to be in between the waters and let a dividing occur between the waters and the waters.' Then God proceeded to make the expanse and to make a division between the waters that should be beneath the expanse and the waters that should be above the expanse. And it came to be so." (Genesis 1:6, 7) Then, on the third day, "God went on to say: 'Let the waters under the heavens be brought together into one place and let the dry land appear.' And it came to be so." —Genesis 1:9.

[48] What the Genesis account says is in full harmony with the description given by the apostle Peter. Because the dry land rose above the surface of the terrestrial water, the 'earth stood compactly out of water.' Yet, by reason of the water surrounding the earth above the expanse (which contained the gases needed for supporting life), the earth also stood "in the midst of water." (Compare Proverbs 8:24-29.) This arrangement came into being by the "word of God."

[49] The waters suspended far above earth's surface and the terrestrial waters created the possibility for a global deluge and did prove to be the means by which the Most High destroyed an ungodly world. Hence, the Flood stands as a warning example to all who ridicule the certainty

---

48. How did the earth come to 'stand compactly out of water' and "in the midst of water"?
49. (a) How was it that "by those means the world of that time suffered destruction"? (b) What future event does the powerful "word of God" make certain?

of divine intervention in human affairs during the time of Christ's presence. The powerful word that brought into being the possibilities for a global deluge is the same word that points to the destruction of the present wicked system of things. The apostle Peter continues: "But by the same word the heavens and the earth that are now are stored up for fire and are being reserved to the day of judgment and of destruction of the ungodly men."—2 Peter 3:7.

⁵⁰ Especially because many centuries have passed since the apostle Peter wrote these words and because certain expectations have been unfulfilled, some persons associated with the Christian congregation have questioned whether such a destruction will ever come. While perhaps not openly joining the ridiculers, they no longer view "the day of judgment" as an event with which they must reckon. They become negligent in living up to their Christian responsibilities, and succumb to a state of spiritual drowsiness. They strive to get as much as possible from the present system of things in the way of pleasures and possessions.

APPRECIATE JEHOVAH'S PATIENCE

⁵¹ From a human standpoint, it may seem that Christ's coming in the capacity of the executioner of divine vengeance has been a long time in arriving. But this has not been true in the eyes of Jehovah God. Consequently, for us to avoid going to sleep spiritually, we need to view matters from

50. (a) With reference to the destruction of the present old system of things, what viewpoint have some persons who are associated with the Christian congregation adopted? (b) How is this attitude being manifested?
51. Why should we not think that Christ's coming in the capacity of an executioner has been a long time in arriving?

the standpoint of the Most High. The apostle Peter's words can help us to do just that. We read:

> "However, let this one fact not be escaping your notice, beloved ones, that one day is with Jehovah as a thousand years and a thousand years as one day. Jehovah is not slow respecting his promise, as some people consider slowness, but he is patient with you because he does not desire any to be destroyed but desires all to attain to repentance. Yet Jehovah's day will come as a thief."—2 Peter 3:8-10.

[52] Jehovah is not indifferent to time as it applies to man. (Genesis 1:14, 15) He made man to be a timekeeper. In the Bible, God has marked out specific time periods, these being measured in years according to man's count of time. (Genesis 15:13-16; Exodus 12:40, 41; Galatians 3:17; Numbers 14:33, 34; 32:13; Deuteronomy 2:7; Joshua 5:6; Acts 13:20) Since he is a God without beginning and end, from eternity to eternity, his own life cannot be measured in time. (Psalm 90:2, 4) So what is to man a thousand years or a period of more than 365,000 days is, comparatively speaking, like just one 24-hour day to the eternal God.

[53] When the inspired Peter says, also, that "one day is with Jehovah as a thousand years," he does not mean that time drags on tiresomely for Jehovah with regard to earthly or human affairs. Rather, in one 24-hour day God could accomplish what it would take man, say, a thousand years to get done. But the Most High is never crowded for time, although he can speed things up. Yet, if he wants to wait a thousand years before taking a certain action, he is waiting only a "day," relatively speaking.

52, 53. How is a thousand years as one day to Jehovah, and one day as a thousand years?

⁵⁴ So, instead of looking at the centuries that have passed since the apostle Peter wrote his second letter as an evidence of slowness on God's part, we should regard this period as a marvelous demonstration of divine patience. It proves undeniably that our heavenly Father wants people everywhere to come to repentance and live. As Peter pointed out, God's patience has benefited Christians. At one time they, too, were unbelievers and needed to repent in order to gain an approved standing with the Most High. However, if divine judgment had been executed against the ungodly world, those who had not yet come to repentance would have perished. Thus Jehovah's patience has allowed for the salvation of Christians, even as it is now continuing to open up opportunities for still others to come to repentance and live. Nevertheless, divine patience will not be shown indefinitely. Unexpectedly, as when a thief comes, the Lord Jesus Christ will be revealed "in a flaming fire" as he begins his work of executing the ungodly.—2 Thessalonians 1:7-9.

⁵⁵ Because such revelation of the Lord Jesus Christ can come at any time, we need to think seriously about our standing before God and Christ. We do not have endless time to build up a record of fine works that will result in our being viewed as approved by them. The Bible clearly shows that our Master's day for judging will overtake those not watchful. If we are negligent about our Christian responsibilities, then, as a thief, such an event could catch us in an unprepared state. Therefore, we should strive to live each day as if

54. (a) Why should we not think of Jehovah God as being slow? (b) How have we benefited from God's patience?
55. What should we be doing in view of the certainty of Christ's coming to execute judgment, and what can this mean for us?

it were our last, not allowing personal desires or pleasures to interfere with our faithfully serving Jehovah God and our Lord Jesus Christ. In that case, we will never regret the way in which we have used our time, our energies and our material assets. The revelation of the Lord Jesus Christ will then not be a time that will expose us as disloyal slaves deserving of punishment. But it will start a period of unparalleled blessings for us as part of the "new heavens" or the "new earth" of God's making. Surely, this is a grand hope that deserves to be safeguarded.—2 Peter 3:13.

11

Live in Expectation of the Fulfillment of the Promise

A WHOLE world order is due to change. Every facet of human living is bound to be affected. This change is inevitable since the unfailing "word of God" has decreed the end of the present heavens and earth and their replacement by glorious new heavens and a new earth. What will these developments mean for us? How can we show that we are living in expectation of the fulfillment of what Jehovah God has promised?

² After referring to the global flood in Noah's days, the apostle Peter writes: "The heavens and the earth that are now are stored up for fire and are being reserved to the day of judgment and of destruction of the ungodly men." (2 Peter 3:7) The apostle goes on to say that "the heavens will pass away with a hissing noise, but the elements being intensely hot will be dissolved, and earth and the works in it will be discovered." —2 Peter 3:10.

³ Based on these inspired words, are we to conclude that our literal earth as well as the sun, moon and stars will be destroyed? To answer this

---

1, 2. (a) What will yet happen according to the changeless "word of God," giving rise to what questions? (b) How does the apostle Peter describe what will happen to the present order?
3. In view of the Genesis account, what must we logically conclude about the material universe, including our earth?

question, we must consider God's view of his own works. With reference to the end of the creative period, the Genesis account tells us: "God saw everything he had made and, look! it was very good." (Genesis 1:31) The prospect before the first humans was an eternity of happy living on earth, provided that they remained obedient. (Genesis 2:16, 17; 3:3) Nothing in the Genesis account implies that the earth would be but a temporary home for man, finally to be destroyed at some future judgment day. It logically follows that God's purpose is for the material universe, including our earth, to continue in unending existence.

4 Moreover, the apostle Peter made a distinction between (1) the "heavens from of old and an earth standing compactly out of water and in the midst of water" and (2) "the heavens and the earth *that are now.*" (2 Peter 3:5, 7) Yet, the earth that existed before the Flood is the same planet that still exists. True, the deluge did bring about changes in the physical features of the earth. Since water was no longer suspended high above earth's surface, this affected the appearance of the visible universe from the standpoint of the human observer. However, these changes were merely side effects of the Flood. Its purpose was not to destroy the *literal planet* but to destroy the *ungodly human society* outside the ark. By means of the deluge, all the works and arrangements that the godless human society had built up perished.

5 Hence, for there to be a correspondency with

4. (a) What distinction did Peter make in connection with the situation before and after the Flood? (b) What did the Flood not do?
5. For there to be a correspondency with the global flood, what must happen at the day of reckoning?

the global flood, everything associated with the present wicked human society must perish, as if consumed by fire. Yes, the entire framework of human affairs that came into existence after the Flood has been reserved for destruction and a day of judgment or reckoning.

⁶ That the "fire" is here used representatively of the thoroughness of the destruction is confirmed in the Bible book of Revelation, where the Lord Jesus Christ is depicted as a warring king. His battle action is said to leave many corpses strewn on earth's surface, to be consumed by scavenger birds. (Revelation 19:15-18) Such a picture could not be fulfilled to any degree if this planet were to be reduced literally to a lifeless cinder.

⁷ So, then, Peter's portrayal of the destruction of the present earth and heavens relates to the annihilation of ungodly human society. Man-made governments that have dominated over human society like "heavens" will pass out of existence. (Compare Isaiah 34:2-5; Micah 1:3, 4.) The sound of their dissolving into ruins, described as a "hissing noise" like that of steam escaping under pressure, will build up in intensity. The "elements," that is, the spirit that motivates ungodly mankind to think, plan, speak and act in their God-dishonoring way will be dissolved or reduced to nothingness. (Compare Acts 9:1; Ephesians 2:1-3.) This will spell the end for all the philosophies, theories, arrangements and schemes that reflect the spirit of mankind alienated from the Most High. "Earth and the works in it will be discovered" or exposed as deserving destruction.

6. Is the "fire," by means of which the old order ends, literal?
7. What do the words of 2 Peter 3:10 indicate about the destruction to come?

There will be no escape for any member of the wicked human society, the "earth." (Compare Genesis 11:1; Isaiah 66:15, 16; Amos 9:1-3; Zephaniah 1:12-18.) All the works of lawless men —the institutions and organizations as well as what has been built up in connection with these— will be revealed as divinely disapproved, to be disposed of as worthless refuse.

⁸ We servants of God, therefore, want to live in a manner showing that we really believe that every part of this present ungodly system will perish everlastingly. This is what the apostle Peter urges us to do, saying:

"Since all these things are thus to be dissolved, what sort of persons ought you to be in holy acts of conduct and deeds of godly devotion, awaiting and keeping close in mind the presence of the day of Jehovah, through which the heavens being on fire will be dissolved and the elements being intensely hot will melt!"—2 Peter 3:11, 12.

⁹ When every part of this system is dissolved by the "fire" of God's anger expressed through the Lord Jesus Christ, only persons with a record of upright conduct and godly devotion will escape. True worship is not passive, reflecting itself solely in a person's abstaining from certain wrongs. While maintaining moral and spiritual purity is essential, we are also under obligation to demonstrate our love for our fellow humans by being willing and eager to respond to their physical and spiritual needs. And this contributes to great joy, for "there is more happiness in giving than there is in receiving."—Acts 20:35.

8. Since every part of the present system will be destroyed, what counsel of Peter should we take to heart?
9. Who only will survive the coming destruction, with everlasting blessings in view?

ACTIONS INDICATING THAT WE
RECOGNIZE THE APPROACHING END

¹⁰ The following words of the apostle Peter amplify what we need to be doing in view of the approaching "end of all things": "Be sound in mind, therefore, and be vigilant with a view to prayers. Above all things, have intense love for one another, because love covers a multitude of sins. Be hospitable to one another without grumbling."—1 Peter 4:7-9.

¹¹ In harmony with this admonition, to remain morally clean or upright in conduct and to be active in promoting the spiritual welfare of others, we need to be "sound in mind." This requires that we guard against letting emotions rule and allowing them to unbalance us mentally. It is vital that we recognize the truly important things in life, that we have a balanced sense of what deserves priority.—Philippians 1:9, 10.

¹² If we want to remain God's faithful servants, we cannot hope to succeed in our own strength. We need to look to Jehovah God for aid, being "vigilant with a view to prayers." From personal experience, the apostle Peter learned the importance of being "vigilant," watchful or alert with reference to prayers. Just prior to Jesus Christ's being arrested by an armed mob in the garden of Gethsemane, the Son of God had encouraged Peter, James and John to pray so that they might not fall victim to temptation. However, all three apostles fell asleep at this critical

10. On account of the approaching "end of all things," what admonition did Peter give?
11. What is needed for us to remain "sound in mind"?
12. (a) Why is it important to be "vigilant with a view to prayers"? (b) How did Peter come to appreciate the importance of this from his own experience?

time. (Matthew 26:36-46; Mark 14:32-42; Luke 22:39-46) Weakened by his failure to remain "vigilant" as regards prayer, Peter later denied Jesus Christ three times. (John 18:17, 18, 25-27) Yet, earlier, Peter had confidently declared: "Lord, I am ready to go with you both into prison and into death." (Luke 22:33) "Although all the others are stumbled in connection with you, never will I be stumbled!"—Matthew 26:33.

[13] There is a vital lesson for us in what happened to Peter. It can impress on us the danger of overconfidence. Because of our limitations and weaknesses, it is only with divine help that we can succeed in resisting temptation. May we, therefore, keep on praying with an alert mind and a heart that is unwavering in its affections for Jehovah God and Jesus Christ.

[14] Besides remaining alert and balanced with reference to Christian discipleship, we do well to consider whether love is motivating us to fulfill our responsibilities. (1 Corinthians 13:1-3) The apostle Peter urged that we have "intense love" for fellow believers. Such intense love is demonstrated by our having a forgiving spirit. When that is the case, we do not exaggerate the faults of our brothers nor do we call undue attention to their failings. We do not look for mistakes, putting the transgressions of others in the worst light possible. In our thus being forgiving, our love will cover a multitude of sins instead of exposing them to full view for others to see.

---

13. What can we learn from Peter's experience when he failed to be "vigilant with a view to prayers"?
14. What should be our motive in fulfilling our Christian responsibility, and how is this manifest in our dealings with our fellow believers?

¹⁵ The showing of hospitality is also an expression of love. How fine it is when we share our food and necessities with others, especially those in need! (Luke 14:12-14) When fellow believers lose everything through natural disasters or persecution, this may mean opening our homes to them for extended periods. This may be very inconvenient for us, and we might tend to complain about the extra demands being put on our assets and energies. At such times we do well to guard against grumbling about having to show hospitality time and again, recognizing that this is a fine way in which we can display our love for those whom God loves.

¹⁶ All of us do have gifts or endowments that we can use for the benefit of others. Our remaining God's approved servants depends on our using these gifts eagerly and cheerfully. Wisely, we would avoid comparing ourselves with others. This can prevent our being discouraged when seeing that others can do much more than we can. On the other hand, we would not give in to any feelings of superiority when we can accomplish more in some field of activity than others can. (Galatians 6:3, 4) Note what the apostle Peter said: "In proportion as each one has received a gift, use it in ministering to one another as fine stewards of God's undeserved kindness expressed in various ways." (1 Peter 4:10) Accordingly, we are responsible to use to the full whatever gifts we may have. By God's undeserved kindness we are what we are and have what we have. Hence,

15. Why may it be necessary to show hospitality, and with what attitude should it be extended?
16, 17. (a) How should we view the gifts that we have? (b) What fine attitude did Paul recommend and manifest himself?

all our energies, abilities and talents may be viewed as gifts that have been granted us by Jehovah's undeserved kindness, to be used to bring praise and honor to the Most High.

¹⁷ The apostle Paul highlighted the right attitude by means of the following questions: "Who makes you to differ from another? Indeed, what do you have that you did not receive? If, now, you did indeed receive it, why do you boast as though you did not receive it?" (1 Corinthians 4:7) Though Paul himself could say that he "labored in excess" of all the other apostles, he did not take the credit to himself but added, "yet not I but the undeserved kindness of God that is with me."—1 Corinthians 15:10.

¹⁸ As faithful stewards, we will want to be concerned about making full use of whatever gifts we may have in helping others spiritually and materially. The *manner* in which we do so is also very important. In this regard, Peter wrote:

"If anyone speaks, let him speak as it were the sacred pronouncements of God; if anyone ministers, let him minister as dependent on the strength that God supplies; so that in all things God may be glorified through Jesus Christ. The glory and the might are his forever and ever. Amen."—1 Peter 4:11.

¹⁹ Hence, if we are helping others spiritually, we will want to speak in such a way as to show that the source of our comforting, loving words is Jehovah God. When that is the case, our preaching and teaching will be upbuilding and will not engender feelings of inferiority and shame in those whom we are striving to aid. Similarly, if

18. In what manner should we be using our gifts?
19. How can we glorify God when helping others spiritually and materially?

we give of our time and energies in rendering physical aid, we will want to rely on God for strength. This would de-emphasize our own abilities and highlight *God's use* of our capacities for doing good. In this way, our heavenly Father will be glorified. (1 Corinthians 3:5-7) Since such glory or honor is given to the Father because of our being disciples of his Son, Jehovah God is "glorified through Jesus Christ." Yes, the Most High is responsible for giving us the ability and the strength to accomplish good.

[20] By using our time, assets and energies to aid others, we show that we are in a state of spiritual preparedness, ready to face the great day of Jehovah. In fact, our recognizing that the Lord Jesus Christ could come at any time as the executioner of divine vengeance can incite us to remain spiritually awake. That is why we want to keep ever before us the certainty of the coming of Jehovah's great day. Because it will open up grand opportunities for all loyal disciples of Jesus Christ, we can rightly look forward to it with eager anticipation. The day of Jehovah will mean being freed forever from the unrighteousness and pressures of the present system of things, to enjoy the blessings of "new heavens and a new earth." How vital it is that we keep this day "close in mind," ardently desiring it! (2 Peter 3:12, 13) Our zealous participation in making known God's purpose to others gives evidence of the proper attitude. It shows that we are convinced that Jehovah's day will come and that others need to know about it and act in harmony with this vital knowledge.

---

20. Why should we look forward to the coming of Jehovah's great day, and so what should we be doing?

[21] God's promise of "new heavens and a new earth," first stated through the prophet Isaiah, will be fulfilled to its fullest significance. (Isaiah 65:17; 66:22) A righteous rule in the hands of Jesus Christ and his associate king-priests over an earthly society conforming to divine law must become a reality. (Revelation 5:9, 10; 20:6) The certainty of this can stir us to action, moving us to do our utmost to be among those who share in the blessings that will result. The apostle Peter admonished: "Beloved ones, since you are awaiting these things, do your utmost to be found finally by him spotless and unblemished and in peace." (2 Peter 3:14) As God's servants, our concern is to be approved by the Lord Jesus Christ, not being spotted or blemished by worldly attitudes, ways and actions. We want to be free from the stain of sin. Since sin disrupts our peace with God, only by remaining in a state where our sins can be atoned for can we be found "in peace" at the coming of his great day.

APPRECIATE DIVINE PATIENCE

[22] While we rightly look forward to "new heavens and a new earth," we do not want to become impatient about the fulfillment of the promise. The fact that Jehovah's great day did not come long ago has allowed for our own salvation. The apostle Peter stated:

> "Consider the patience of our Lord as salvation, just as our beloved brother Paul according to the wisdom given him also wrote you, speaking about these things as he does also in all his letters. In them, however, are some things hard to understand,

21. (a) Of what can we be sure in connection with God's promise of "new heavens and a new earth"? (b) How should this affect us?
22. Why should we not become impatient about the fulfillment of God's promise?

which the untaught and unsteady are twisting, as they do also the rest of the Scriptures, to their own destruction."—2 Peter 3:15, 16.

²³ As persons who appreciate Jehovah's patience, we will want to be careful not to presume on it, justifying a particular course of selfishness on the basis that God's great day may yet be far away. In the first century C.E., there were believers who apparently did this. The apostle Peter describes them as "untaught and unsteady," lacking a clear understanding of God's Word and being unstable with reference to Christian doctrine and practice. These persons even tried to use statements from the letters of the inspired apostle Paul and other parts of the Scriptures to excuse their wrong conduct. It may be that they pointed to what Paul had written about the exercise of conscience and about being declared righteous by faith and not by works of the Mosaic law as providing latitude for all kinds of actions that were contrary to God's will. (Compare Romans 3:5-8; 6:1; 7:4; 8:1, 2; Galatians 3:10.) They may have misused such points as the following:

"Christ set us free. Therefore stand fast, and do not let yourselves be confined again in a yoke of slavery." (Galatians 5:1) "All things are lawful for me." (1 Corinthians 6:12) "All things are clean to clean persons." (Titus 1:15)

However, they ignored that Paul also said:

"Do not use this freedom as an inducement for the flesh, but through love slave for one another. For the entire Law stands fulfilled in one saying, namely: 'You must love your neighbor as yourself.'" (Galatians 5:13, 14) "Let each one keep seeking, not his own advantage, but that of the other person."—1 Corinthians 10:24.

---

23. (a) Why should we not presume on God's patience? (b) How did some in the first century fail to recognize the reason for God's patience?

²⁴ As in the first-century congregation, so today there are those who would extend the limits of Christian freedom to the point of becoming enslaved to sin. Therefore, we do well to guard our associations, lest we come under unwholesome influence and be led astray. Calling attention to this fact, the apostle Peter wrote: "You, therefore, beloved ones, having this advance knowledge, be on your guard that you may not be led away with them by the error of the law-defying people and fall from your own steadfastness."—2 Peter 3:17.

MAKE ADVANCEMENT AS A CHRISTIAN

²⁵ To avoid losing out on the blessings that Jehovah God has in store for us, we should want to make progress in Christian living and activity. (2 Peter 3:18) Our doing so harmonizes with the apostle Peter's encouragement:

"Yes, for this very reason, by your contributing in response all earnest effort, supply to your faith virtue, to your virtue knowledge, to your knowledge self-control, to your self-control endurance, to your endurance godly devotion, to your godly devotion brotherly affection, to your brotherly affection love." —2 Peter 1:5-7.

²⁶ Through his Son, Jehovah God has given us the capacity for *faith*. Hence, in response to, or as a consequence of, what has been done in our behalf, we should want to develop other fine qualities that give evidence of our having genuine faith. This we do by letting God's Word and his spirit exert their full force in our lives. (2 Peter 1:1-4) The apostle Peter admonished that we

24. Why must we guard our associations even inside the congregation?
25, 26. After obtaining faith, what should we be doing in harmony with 2 Peter 1:5-7?

'contribute all earnest effort,' exerting ourselves diligently with all the strength that we have, in cooperating with the work our heavenly Father is doing in making us complete Christians.—Compare 1 Corinthians 3:6, 7; James 1:2-4.

²⁷ Our adding *virtue* to faith means striving to be persons of moral excellence in imitation of our Exemplar, Christ. Such virtue or moral excellence is a positive quality. Its possessor not only refrains from doing bad or causing injury to his fellowmen but also seeks to do good, responding positively to the spiritual, physical and emotional needs of others.

²⁸ Moral excellence cannot exist apart from *knowledge*. We need knowledge to distinguish right from wrong. (Hebrews 5:14) It is also essential for evaluating just how positive good is to be expressed in a given situation. (Philippians 1:9, 10) Unlike credulity, which makes light of or even resists knowledge, solidly based faith rests on and always benefits from knowledge. Hence, our being diligent in applying the Holy Scriptures will strengthen our faith as we continue to grow in knowledge of Jehovah God and his Son.

²⁹ This knowledge serves to restrain us from giving in to sinful passions, becoming immoderate and unbridled in conduct, or in other ways becoming guilty of a serious failure to reflect the divine image in attitude, word and action. Knowledge contributes to our having *self-control,* the ability to bridle one's person, actions and speech.

---

27. What is meant by adding virtue to our faith?
28. Why is it important to grow in knowledge?
29. (a) Why is knowledge essential in cultivating self-control? (b) What is the relationship between self-control and endurance?

By continuing to exercise self-control, we will have the essential quality of *endurance*. The inner strength that endurance produces can also help us to resist giving in to sinful passions, compromising when suffering persecution or becoming preoccupied with daily cares, pleasures or material possessions. This endurance stems from relying on the Most High for strength and guidance. —Compare Philippians 4:12, 13; James 1:5.

³⁰ *Godly devotion* or reverentialness should be added to endurance. Such an attitude distinguishes the entire life course of a genuine Christian. It manifests itself in a wholesome regard and honor for the Creator and a deep respect and concern for parents or others to whom devotion is due. (1 Timothy 5:4) Without *brotherly affection,* however, godliness cannot exist. The apostle John stated:

"If anyone makes the statement: 'I love God,' and yet is hating his brother, he is a liar. For he who does not love his brother, whom he has seen, cannot be loving God, whom he has not seen." (1 John 4:20)

Anyone priding himself on his reverence and devotion would still be woefully lacking if he failed to show affection, kindness and friendliness to his brothers. We cannot be warm toward God and cool toward our brothers.

³¹ *Love* is the outstanding quality that should be especially evident in our lives. This kind of love is not to be limited to our Christian brothers. While we are to have affection for our spiritual brothers, love is to be shown to all mankind.

30. (a) What is godly devotion, and how does it manifest itself? (b) What shows that godliness cannot exist apart from brotherly affection?
31. To whom should love be shown, and why?

This love is not dependent on the moral standing of the individual. It is to be shown even toward enemies, particularly expressing itself in a desire to help them spiritually.—Matthew 5:43-48.

[32] What results when virtue, knowledge, self-control, endurance, godly devotion, brotherly affection and love are added to faith? The apostle Peter answers: "If these things exist in you and overflow, they will prevent you from being either inactive or unfruitful regarding the accurate knowledge of our Lord Jesus Christ." (2 Peter 1:8) We will then not be standing still, inactive, dead spiritually. With godly qualities lodging in our hearts, being truly a part of us, we will be motivated to think, speak and act in a divinely approved way. (Compare Luke 6:43-45.) When this is true in our case, the coming of the Lord Jesus Christ to take full control of earth's affairs will be the start of blessings far grander than we can now imagine.

[33] May we, therefore, never become careless in our conduct or in the discharge of our Christian responsibilities, including the vital work of making known God's message to others. If we have chosen a life as disciples of Jesus Christ we can enjoy a clean conscience and wholesome companionship with fellow believers. We can experience God's strengthening aid in times of trial, and our relationship with others will improve as we conscientiously apply Bible principles.

[34] There is not an area of life—at home, on the job, in our dealings with governmental authorities on all levels—that will not be affected for good if we strive to follow God's Word. It will also make

---

32. What results when we apply the counsel of 2 Peter 1:5-7?
33-35. How do we benefit from living as disciples of Jesus Christ?

us more aware of the importance of being whole-hearted in reaching as many people as possible with the Bible's comforting message. We will find great happiness and a true sense of accomplishment in responding to the needs of our fellow humans, especially to their spiritual needs.

[35] Most important of all, living as genuine disciples of Jesus Christ is the only course that holds promise of an eternal future of happy living. Surely we would not want to lose what we have gained. May the passing of each day find us in a state of readiness for the coming of our Master in the capacity of a completely victorious king. Only then can we share in the boundless joy resulting from our having chosen to stick to our commitment to serve Jehovah God faithfully.

For further information write WATCHTOWER at an address given below

ALASKA 99507: 2552 East 48th Ave., Anchorage. AUSTRALIA: 11 Beresford Road, Strathfield, N.S.W. 2135. BAHAMAS: Box N-1247, Nassau, N.P. BARBADOS: Fontabelle Rd., Bridgetown. BELIZE: Box 257, Belize City. BRAZIL: Rua Guaíra, 216, Bosque da Saúde, 04142 São Paulo, SP; Caixa Postal 12.896, 01000 São Paulo, SP. CANADA M6A 1Z5: 150 Bridgeland Ave., Toronto, Ont. ENGLAND: Watch Tower House, The Ridgeway, London NW7 1RN. FIJI: Box 23, Suva. FRANCE: 81 rue du Point-du-Jour, 92100 Boulogne-Billancourt. GERMANY, FEDERAL REPUBLIC OF: Postfach 5920, D-6200 Wiesbaden 1. GHANA: Box 760, Accra. GUYANA: 50 Brickdam, Georgetown 16. HAWAII 96814: 1228 Pensacola St., Honolulu. HONG KONG: 312 Prince Edward Rd., Second Floor, Kowloon. INDIA: Post Bag 10, Lonavla, Pune Dis., Mah. 410 401. IRELAND: 86 Lindsay Rd., Glasnevin, Dublin 9. JAMAICA: 41 Trafalgar Rd., Kingston 10. KENYA: Box 47788, Nairobi. LEEWARD ISLANDS: Box 119, St. Johns, Antigua. LIBERIA: P.O. Box 171, Monrovia. MALAYSIA: 20 Scotland Close, Penang. NEWFOUNDLAND, CANADA A1C 2M1: 239 Pennywell Rd., St. John's. NEW ZEALAND: 6-A Western Springs Rd., Auckland 3. NIGERIA: P.O. Box 194, Yaba, Lagos State. PAKISTAN: 8-E Habibullah Rd., Lahore 3. PANAMA: Apartado 1386, Panama 1. PAPUA NEW GUINEA: Box 113, Port Moresby. PHILIPPINES, REPUBLIC OF: P.O. Box 2044, Manila 2800; 186 Roosevelt Ave., San Francisco del Monte, Quezon City 3010. PORTUGAL: Apartado 91, P-2766 Estoril Codex. RHODESIA: 35 Fife Avenue, Salisbury. SIERRA LEONE: Box 136, Freetown. SOUTH AFRICA: Private Bag 2, Elandsfontein, 1406. SRI LANKA, REP. OF: 62 Layard's Road, Colombo 5. SWITZERLAND: Ulmenweg 45; P.O. Box 477, CH-3601 Thun. TRINIDAD: 2 La Seiva Road, Maraval, Port of Spain. UNITED STATES OF AMERICA: 117 Adams St., Brooklyn, N.Y. 11201.